ISBN 978-1-330-27651-8
PIBN 10010416

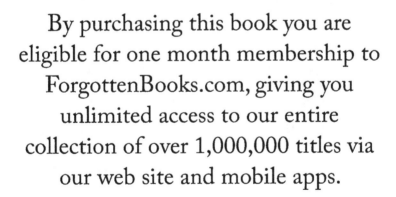

English
Français
Deutsche
Italiano
Español
Português

www.forgottenbooks.com

Mythology Photography **Fiction**
Fishing Christianity **Art** Cooking
Essays Buddhism Freemasonry
Medicine **Biology** Music **Ancient
Egypt** Evolution Carpentry Physics
Dance Geology **Mathematics** Fitness
Shakespeare **Folklore** Yoga Marketing
Confidence Immortality Biographies
Poetry **Psychology** Witchcraft
Electronics Chemistry History **Law**
Accounting **Philosophy** Anthropology
Alchemy Drama Quantum Mechanics
Atheism Sexual Health **Ancient History**
Entrepreneurship Languages Sport
Paleontology Needlework Islam
Metaphysics Investment Archaeology
Parenting Statistics Criminology
Motivational

CLERGY AND CHOIR.

— BY THE —

REV. CHARLES R. HODGE,

Of the Diocese of Chicago.

MILWAUKEE:

THE YOUNG CHURCHMAN CO.

1891.

CONTENTS.

TO

MY CLERICAL BRETHREN,

WHO ARE SO OFTEN ENGAGED

IN WRESTLING WITH THE

"CHOIR PROBLEM,"

•THIS ATTEMPT

AT A SOLUTION

IS

𝔖𝔶𝔪𝔭𝔞𝔱𝔥𝔢𝔱𝔦𝔠𝔞𝔩𝔩𝔶 𝔍𝔫𝔰𝔠𝔯𝔦𝔟𝔢𝔡

BY

THE AUTHOR.

PREFACE.

The following extracts are copied from letters received at various times, within the past two or three years, from certain of my brethren of the clergy, whose reasons for writing thus to me are doubtless sufficient and satisfactory to themselves:

"I need your advice, ever so much, about our choir. Nothing serious, but they *don't get on*, in a musical way."

"My first and—so far—only conflict, has been with my choir—a very fine quartette, by the way. At the rehearsal for my first Sunday's service, I thought I would go around to the church and give them a list of the hymns that I wanted sung for that Sunday. I thought that I detected a certain indefinable air of—well, of resentment about it; at least I was told that it was the custom of my predecessor to allow the choir to choose their own hymns for Sunday services. I declined to be guided by Mr. M——'s custom, not particularly caring to have a sermon on "repentance" followed or preceded by a hymn on "the Holy Scriptures," or on "Praise," or "Heaven." I wonder what you would have done under the circumstances—I presume you would have done as I did. I referred them to the Canon on Church Music, which is printed in the front of the hymnal they use, and told them that such was the law of the Church, by which clergy, choir and laity in general are bound."

"How am I to get my choir to sing as they ought? More particularly the men; the women do well enough. Their voices don't seem to *harmonize*."

"If I should decide on having a vested choir, *where could I put them?* You know my church well enough to know that the chancel is altogether too small for such a choir; it would have to be enlarged—but how? Please draw me a plan, or, better still, run down here for a day."

"You remember the boy I had to scold the Sunday you were here? I have trouble of the same sort with him continually. What would you do with him?"

"How does the 'Choir Club' get on? Tell me something about it, or send me a copy of the Constitution."

I could present many more, but these will suffice. Such letters, as well as frequent oral requests for counsel on the many phases of the "choir problem," finally induced me to attempt the preparation of a series of letters of advice, upon all possible cases that would come to my mind. Very early in its preparation the epistolary form was abandoned, on account of its clumsiness, and the result is the following pages.

Nothing but the manifest need of such a work would induce this venture on my part; nor would even that excuse it, were it not for the long and intimate experience, both as boy and man, with choirs of all descriptions and varieties at its back. And again, it has been represented to me that the fruits of such an experience as mine has been, in this matter, ought not to be regarded as my private property, and this representation has also had its influence.

There is nothing in the entire range of Church literature, to my knowledge, which touches upon all these points. The few books that have been published on the subject of Vested Choirs are excellent; but they all appear to take for granted, as being well understood, certain points on which there is, in reality, dense ignorance.

In conclusion, I must express my obligations, as also my sincere thanks, to two of my brethren, for contributions, at my request, on certain phases of "the problem," which will be found in their proper places, duly accredited.

If this book will, in course of time, be found helpful to any of my brethren, it will have fully accomplished the purpose designed in its preparation.

CHARLES R. HODGE.

Grace Church Rectory,
New Lenox, Ill.
Feast of the Circumcision of Christ [Jan. 1], 1891.

CLERGY AND CHOIR.

CHAPTER I.

INTRODUCTORY.

The average parish priest will acknowledge, without hesitation, that the music in his services is at times a source of trouble and perplexity. By the canon law of the Church, not only the hymns, but also the tunes, are placed under his control. This latter, however, he may, and generally does, relegate to some musical person, satisfied if the music moves on smoothly, and is not glaringly out of place.

In the canon referred to, and which we shall presently examine, there is evident a dim idea that the clergyman should be possessed of some musical abilities or tastes, enough, at least, to enable him to judge as to the fitness of certain music for the "service of the sanctuary." But, unfortunately, the clergyman who is "not at all musical" is not at all rare, and he occasionally finds himself in situations of considerable discomfort, being placed in charge of a matter upon which he is compelled to accept the judgment of others, and in which inclinations and tastes must be consulted, although he has none of his own.

The wisest course for such a clergyman to pursue is to find some sober and discreet person possessed of the needful musical qualifications, and confide in him. It is best that such confidant should not be one of the choir, and should be a man, rather than a woman; not necessarily a trained musician—indeed it is better otherwise—but possessed of a musical ear, a love for music, a sound, matured judgment in ordinary matters, and, above all, "sober and discreet." The relations between the clergyman and his confidant, on this point, it need hardly be said, should be strictly confidential.

But, though the clergyman be not unmusical, though he be even musically gifted in ear, voice and taste, he is still in an uncomfortable position. He knows little or nothing about choirs and their training, unless, as is occasionally the case, he has been a member of a choir as a layman. He has no special training in this direction, and has very vague—if any—ideas of the Church's musical heritage. Generally, beyond a misty notion or so to the effect that "operatic music ought not to be sung in church," and that "Gospel Hymns" do not represent the highest standard of either music or Churchliness, he has no guidance save what he obtains piecemeal from his seniors in orders, in scraps from his musical friends, and stray items and occasional articles in the Church periodicals.

It sometimes happens that the young clergyman is sent to a field to inaugurate a new work, to establish the Church in a place where it is practically unknown. One of the first problems confronting him is the music, and he finds himself thrown upon his own resources in attempting its solution. But he manfully goes to work and secures a few singers whom he proceeds to organize into a choir, only to discover in a short time that he has succeeded in gathering together certain uneasy elements, once portions of the other choirs in the vicinity, who had dropped out of those choirs from jealousy, pique, injured feelings, natural want of stability, and other kindred reasons ; these natural traits begin to manifest themselves after the novelty has worn off, and the young clergyman finds himself choirless, and is obliged to set himself to work to form another choir, wasting time and labor that might and should be given to other duties. But he has gained a valuable fund of experience, if he is wise enough to use it properly.

And it is not the young clergyman alone who encounters difficulties of this nature, nor are they confined to new fields of labor. The aged priest, after a quarter of a century of continuous labor in one parish, will find the choir problem suddenly starting up and confronting him as lively and vigorous as ever, years after he had congratulated himself that it was safely and finally disposed of ; its life and vigor are perennial, and its presence is universal.

There is no arbitrary or specific manner of meeting these difficulties. *Experientia docet.* But the directions and advice, the reflections and ideas contained in the following pages may be of profit, based, as they are, on some thirty years almost continuous experience in choirs in the various capacities of choir-boy, tenor, director, organist, choirmaster; and, finally, some ten years of priesthood spent in active parochial work, in which the choir problem, in its many phases, has presented itself for solution over and over again.

For convenience, I shall address myself in the following pages to my brother clergymen, especially to those who are musically, as well as otherwise, capable of directing their own music. But the greater part will be of interest to all, I trust. And it may be that some who read it may regard the ideas as of sufficient importance to hand the book over to their choirmasters, with a request to read carefully and profit thereby.

CHAPTER II.

THE CANON ON CHURCH MUSIC.

Digest of Canons: Title I. Canon xxiii. *Sec. 1.*—The Selections of the Psalms in Metre, and Hymns, which are set forth by authority, and Anthems in the words of Holy Scripture [and the Book of Common Prayer] are allowed to be sung in all Congregations of this Church before and after Morning and Evening Prayer, and also before and after Sermons, at the discretion of the Minister, whose duty it shall be, by standing directions, or from time to time, to appoint such authorized Psalms, Hymns, or Anthems as are to be sung.

Sec. 2.—It shall be the duty of every minister of this Church, with such assistance as he may see fit to employ from persons skilled in music, to give order concerning the tunes to be sung at any time in his Church ; and especially it shall be his duty to suppress all light and unseemly music, and all indecency and irreverence in the performance, by which vain and ungodly persons profane the service of the sanctuary.

This canon was adopted in General Convention in 1874; later legislation added in effect the bracketed words in Sec. 1.

A strict compliance with the letter of this law in the first section would deprive many choirs of much of their favorite music. Spohr's "How pleasant, how divinely fair," Woodward's "The radiant morn hath passed away," Sheppard's " 'Forward !' said the prophet," and much oratorio music would be forbidden. It would be wise for our General Convention to concede more liberty in this regard.

In some dioceses it seems to be generally understood that what is sung in the Bishop's church, or Cathedral, is allowable throughout his diocese. The Bishop's right to compose and set forth forms of prayer, or thanksgiving for special occasions, as provided for in Title I, Canon xv, Sec. 13, is good ground for the assumption that he has the right to set forth hymns and anthems other than is provided for in this Canon. The whole matter will some day demand adjustment, and the probable result will be some such arrangement as prevails in England.

But it is the second section of this Canon with which we are specially concerned. It is the minister who has the direction of the *tunes* to be sung, "with such assistance as he may see fit to employ from persons skilled in music;" and it is made his special duty "to suppress all light and unseemly music, and all indecency and irreverence in the performance" of *any* music, "by which vain and ungodly persons profane the service of the sanctuary."

Inasmuch as "light and unseemly," and "vain and ungodly," are not strictly defined in the Canon, it is objected by some that this second section is vague and unsatisfactory. This objection, however, is unreasonable; this is one of the clearest and most positive laws in the entire digest. The clergyman is responsible for his service in every particular, down to the minutest detail, and therefore the Church law very properly makes him the judge of the music in the service of his Church, and his decision is final. He is to say whether he regards the music as "light and unseemly," and to see that it be rendered with due decency and reverence. The choir constitute his assistants in the service; and we may even go beyond the letter of the Canon, and maintain that those assistants should, under no circumstances, be "vain and ungodly" persons. There are very many singers who fall into the mistake of Ahimaaz.*

As to the character of the music, there are some selections which naturally fall into the category of "light and unseemly." The word "light," as here used, means trivial; it does not mean simple. Some of the most devotional and churchly music is simple, but not light, in the canonical sense. And, again, there is music which is not light—neither simple nor trivial—but which is decidedly unseemly, or out of place, sometimes by force of association, as is the case with operatic selections. To illustrate: there are many noble characters in the theatrical profession, and, I doubt not, many godly men among actors; still, for some well-known actor to appear in a prominent position in the services of the Church, arrayed in the Church's vestments, would be painfully incongruous and unseemly. Some actors have indeed become clergymen, but when they did so, they had forsaken their former calling; such is not the case with this class of music. "Solo profugo rejetto," is often sung to sacred words, but it has not forsaken the opera of "Marta;" you are sure to hear it whenever you hear that opera. But there are

---

* See Chapter xix.

fewer such adaptations than there used to be, nor are they so decidedly unseemly as they once were; I can distinctly remember hearing "Sun of my soul," sung to Offenbach's "Saber song," from "La Grande Duchesse."

This canon, more especially its second section, is a just and commonsense one, and should be enforced everywhere. The priest must have control of his own music; it is a part of his service, for which he is as responsible as he is for his sermon; and though he may temporarily relegate that control to "persons skilled in music," when necessity arises he must unhesitatingly exercise his lawful authority. That is the *only* solution of one of the many phases of the choir problem.

CHAPTER III.

CONGREGATIONAL SINGING.

Unquestionably the ideal service of the Church is that in which all the people join with heart and voice—the fulfilment of the Psalmist's outburst, "Let the people praise Thee, O God ; yea, let all the people praise Thee!" This being beyond all dispute, is it not singular that so few efforts are made to improve the singing of the people?

I have attended several churches which had a reputation for excellent congregational singing, and have always found the reputation well deserved ; the singing being excellent, as far as it went ; but it was always confined to metrical hymn tunes.

I have yet to hear a chant sung acceptably—musically speaking—by a parish congregation ; and I have yet to hear even the faintest rumor of any such congregation attempting an anthem or a set piece, although both could be well done.

Surely it is not impossible to devise some practicable method by which the entire congregation may be trained in the musical services of the Church. It has to my knowledge been approximated in a few instances. I know of one priest who serves a small rural congregation on

Sunday afternoons, where there is neither Sunday School nor choir. He catechizes the congregation once a month, and on all the other Sundays prefaces his services by a fifteen minutes' practice in congregational singing. The result is excellent.

Another parish priest of my acquaintance, during one winter that I spent largely in his parish, initiated a plan which I believe would work well if carried out as it might be. He instituted a practice in congregational singing, which he asked me to direct, at the beginning of every Wednesday evening service. But the practice was confined exclusively to metrical tunes and the chants in the Evening Prayer. It resulted in the nearest approach to good chanting that I ever heard from a congregation. Another unforeseen, but valuable, result was the perceptible increase in the size of the Wednesday evening congregations, especially among the young.

Why should not one evening in the week, or a part of an evening, be devoted to this work ? Train the congregation in singing, just as you would train a choir, to a certain extent; first in metrical tunes, then in chants, Gregorian and Anglican ; finally, in some easy settings of the TE DEUM, such as Steggall in A, or the old, familiar Jackson in F, even singing antiphonally, according to the markings in Novello's edition of those settings. Persistent work of this nature would soon tell. With a well-trained vested choir of men and boys, an occasional easy strain (say, an unison) in an anthem, in which the congregation should be thus trained to unite, would be magnificent in its effect. There is nothing visionary or impracticable in this idea.

The first fault usually found with congregational singing is the universal tendency to drag. "Large bodies move slowly." This fault may be remedied by having a director who will, at all practices, beat time for the people, and insist on the congregation following his time. If they are singing with no choir to lead, this beating time should be done at service also. Sometimes a cornet is used in leading, which is very good in keeping up the time. This, however, should only be used in large buildings, well filled; the cornettist should always play the air, or soprano part of the music, and should thoroughly understand his work, especially realizing that he is not playing in a brass band.* For congregational singing, the music of the chants should not be changed often. The same chants, in the main, may be carried through Easter and Ascension tides; then new tunes for Trinity tide, changing, perhaps, in the middle of the season. Advent and Lent require different music, simple and familiar, both in chant and metrical tunes.

But the clergyman may not be able to carry out the ideas here advanced, and yet desire the best congregational singing he can obtain from his people. In that case, he must see that the choir sing at each service one or two familiar hymn tunes, and that the chants are not often

---

* See Appendix F.

changed ; he must also frequently urge his people to sing heartily. In singing the Canticles or the Psalms with a large vested choir to lead, it is well to call occasional attention to the antiphonal feature of the singing, and ask the congregation to observe it, requesting that portion of the congregation on the right side of the centre alley to sing with the choir on that side, and those on the left, to sing with the choir on their side. A very little labor of this kind will enable an ordinary congregation to become as well versed in this feature of the music as the choir itself, and they will much better appreciate and enjoy their own singing.

CHAPTER IV.

In congregational singing, in order to avoid confusion, and to properly observe the Apostolic injunction, "Let all things be done decently and in order," it is necessary to provide some kind of leadership, which may be vested either in an individual, or in that body of trained singers which is termed a choir.

The individual leader should possess a powerful voice of good compass and quality; his position should be in easy sight of the congregation, at some elevated place near the people. He should direct with baton, keeping strict time in metrical and all other tunes in which the time is rhythmic. In chants, he can indicate with baton all pauses and breathing places in recitative, and strictly mark the time in the cadences.

If the congregation is trained to sing in antiphon, as mentioned in the preceding chapter, it would be well for the leader to have at least two aids, or lieutenants, one on each side, to take their places in the congregation, but as near him as possible; these should possess strong voices, and should generally sing the air.

But by far the most effective leadership is that of a

good choir ; and this should always be held to be the chief, and indeed the only true, office of any choir—to lead the people in common praise.

"The Canticles and 'Psalms, and Hymns, and Spiritual Songs' are not to be listened to, not for display. * * * Better have no choir at all than one that would take the words of common praise out of the mouths of the people by rendering it impossible for them to join in it. * * * The choir may, indeed, have its anthem, provided it be worthy. No music can be too grand and lofty for God's service. * * Its [the choir's] office is not to appropriate, but to lead the peoples' praises."* These are wholesome words, as are also the following :

"We recognize the growth of what seems an unwholesome and altogether unwarrantable invasion of congregational privilege and duty. The number is increasing of choirs that virtually capture and possess themselves of the entire liturgic music. You shall attempt to worship in Church after Church, where you find yourself constrained to unbroken silence, unless it is permitted to catch the breath at a choral 'Amen.' The worship is snatched from the lips of the people, and cribbed, and confined fast prisoner within the limits of choir and sanctuary.

"Our purpose is to aid and promote, in every possible way, the restoration of the peoples' worship to its ancient and divinely appointed place in the Lord's House. Worshipping by deputy is a very unsatisfactory and

---

* From Bishop Spalding's "The Best Mode of Working a Parish." p. 66.

indefeasible expedient. While the devotional mood may be helped and fed by listening to an occasional anthem or motette, worshipping *by the ear* is not the normal and divinely appointed way. Every believing, loving heart must find a voice, or its devotion suffers chill and even asphyxiation. The Psalms teach us all this, throughout. We are not only to work out our own salvation, but we are to perform our own personal worship, precisely as we train and educate a personal faith, with personal graces.

"We shall not get down to the bed-rock of this liturgic-worship question, until the people, brought again from the dead, and resuscitated in newness of life, once more respond to the heart-beat, and find a voice for praise and thanksgiving. Then the versicles will slough off their conventional insincerities, and when the priest exclaims: 'O Lord, open Thou our lips,' the 'people' will know what it all means, that they are to lend a part in the sublime office; and they will give the response, *ex animo*, 'And our mouth, (not the choir-mouth) shall show forth Thy praise.'"*

Many choirs do not realize that the monopolizing of all the music by a choir is every whit as unjust to the congregation as the monopoly of all the best music by a soloist would be to the choir.

Of course, the only choir which is distinctively churchly in its structure is that which is composed entirely of men, or of men and boys, arrayed in the

---

* From *The Living Church.*

proper vestments of the Church. This form of choir is available to almost every parish. In some places, however, although available, it is not expedient. For instance, where no competent director can be found—that is, competent in discipline, as well as in musical, intellectual, and moral culture—it would be unwise to attempt such a choir, however plentiful the material. If the clergyman himself is not especially fond of boys, able to enter heartily into their plans and enjoyments, and is not sure of his ability to govern them absolutely and autocratically, he should not undertake the personal direction of such a choir, however competent he might be musically. While a moderately good choir of men and boys is better than the best choir of any other kind, from a churchly stand-point, it is undeniably true that a poor choir of this kind is, from the same standpoint, the very poorest and most intolerable of all choirs.

Where it is impossible or inexpedient to have a vested choir, other kinds of choirs may be formed. A chorus of mixed—male and female—voices, or a quartette, or, in absence of any other material, a quartette or chorus of female voices only, will constitute a choir which can acceptably lead the congregation in the music of the Church's worship.

But, if the Church would be true to her own teaching, this one point can not be too strenuously urged, too strongly impressed upon the choir, individually, and *en masse,* that the duty of the choir is to *lead* the congregation in singing, and not to entertain them : to lift their voices in praise to God, not to an audience. There are an abundance of places to which people may and do resort to hear an eloquent speaker, and to be entertained by artistic and, often, sensuous music ; but the Church of the living God should be no such place. "We assemble and meet together to render thanks for the great benefits we have received at His hands, *to set forth His most worthy praise,* to hear His most holy Word, and to ask those things which are requisite and necessary, as well for the body as the soul." These familiar words of the Church, so often heard without a thought of their meaning—their unwavering protest against the modern popular idea of going to church to hear the preaching and singing—set forth not only the Church's ideal of public worship, but also plain and commonsense directions for fully realizing that ideal.

Special opportunities are often given for forcible presentation of this important truth to our choirs. On a certain occasion, an elaborate programme of music having been prepared by the choir, from some cause or other, a very small congregation was present. One. of the young ladies of the choir suggested the advisability of changing the music, reserving the best of it until a greater number of people should be present to hear and enjoy it. "By no means," said the rector ; "you are not supposed to be singing to a congregation, but to God. He is present where even two or three are gathered together in His name ; and we will present to Him what we have prepared."

Another incident which occurred in one of our larger cities may be cited, illustrative of the same idea. The President of the United States was to be in that city over Sunday, and had expressed his desire and intention of going to a certain Church to participate in divine worship, and incidentally to hear its noted vested choir. Just previous to the procession, the choir master very naturally urged the choir to their best endeavors; "remember," he impressively said, "the President of the United States is present at this service." "And by the way," interrupted the rector, with equal impressiveness and with great solemnity, "you may as well remember that GOD is present also at this service."

"It is sometimes allowed the choir to select an elaborate setting for the TE DEUM, and to sing an anthem, or an offertory sentence, as an offering of their musical skill to the Giver of their talent, a very appropriate and devout custom when it is kept within due limits."* To which we may add that there are times and occasions when a very elaborate service may properly be used entire by a choir capable of rendering it adequately, in which the congregation necessarily has the minimum of singing. But *no* service should be used in which the people have absolutely no voice. Even in the most elaborate setting of the Eucharistic Office, at least "Old Hundred" might be sung at the Presentation of Alms. Such occasions, however, are the exceptions, and more will be said about them in a later chapter.

---

* Church Cyclopædia, Article "Choir."

CHAPTER V.

The choir with which we are most familiar in this country is what is called the Volunteer Mixed Choir, composed of adult male and female voices, and comprising any number of singers above a quartette. The organist is usually, as in other choirs, a paid functionary, and frequently the director, even when he is not the organist, is also under salary.

As this choir is usually composed of ladies and gentlemen who can give no more than one evening in the week to practice, some of whom enter it as much for recreation as from any other motive, its music is not generally of so pretentious a nature as that of other choirs. Still, this choir may, under good direction, do most excellent work, and properly render the music of the service.

This is probably, all things considered, the most available choir. In almost every community can be found a number of good voices that are capable of being trained in the music of the Church, and in sufficient numbers to produce a good volume of tone, and present in due balance the four parts in the harmony.

In forming such a choir, it is wise to bear in mind

that the very qualities which characterize, and indeed even *make* the singer, tend to make him exquisitely sensitive to other things at times. Forgetting or ignoring this important fact, has often been productive of trouble and jealousy in choirs of this kind.

The choir should be formed in the beginning with great care. Do not go to work in a hap-hazard way, asking everyone you learn is a singer to become a member of your choir. Proceed carefully and cautiously. It is a very good plan to first secure one soprano singer upon whom you are reasonably certain you can rely, and consult with her in regard to the other singers. Invite no one without sufficiently consulting those who have already accepted, to ascertain beyond a reasonable doubt that those whom you wish to invite will be acceptable to all. The adoption of this plan, although it may involve a little trouble on your part, will preclude one great source of choir trouble. Another source may be avoided by making it clear that you require other qualifications beside music—that you will not tolerate ill-behavior or disorder.

If the clergyman is not musical, he must first of all select his choirmaster, or director; then, in company with that person, let him proceed as above outlined. In forming a new choir, it is better for invitations to membership to come from the clergyman; but undoubtedly there are circumstances under which he may place the entire matter in the hands of a trustworthy person, and not concern himself at all over it. In such a case, he is to be heartily congratulated.

The choir being formed, the next step is the first practice ; and in outlining this practice we will suppose the choir, as a body, to be ignorant of the Church services and methods of song.

Hymnals must be provided, of course. The best hymnal for general use in such a choir, as containing the greatest number of familiar hymn tunes and a good selection of chants, is Hutchins'. Begin the practice with a few of the most familiar metrical tunes, such as Hebron, Uxbridge and Duke Street. Let these be sung with little or no comment, except what encouragement you can give and such praise as you can conscientiously bestow. Then select one or two hymns for the first service at which the choir is to sing, and. let them be set to familiar tunes. A laudable ambition may be aroused at this practice by attempting some tune beyond their present capacity; such tunes are easily found; hymns 68, 76, 144, 189 (first), or 512 [Hutchins] will answer the purpose. When they fail in singing it, say to them, "We are not up to this kind of music yet, but it will not be long before we will sing it, and even more difficult music."

If the choir is needed for immediate service, it would be advisable—maybe, even necessary—to read the *Venite* and other Psalms and Canticles in the service, until they are sufficiently trained to sing them properly. The *Venite* and *Jubilate* [or *Benedictus*] could be sung before the TE

DEUM is learned. In Evening Prayer, the shortest chants, *Bonum Est* and *Nunc Dimittis,* might be learned first.

Instruction in chanting should begin at the very outset. Take the *Gloria Patri* first; write it on a blackboard, or previously write it on pieces of music paper, to some melodious and easy single [Anglican] chant, but *not* in chant form—for example, take the following chant, by Medley, writing it thus:

Explain the structure of the chant as here written : it consists of two parts, recitative and cadence, two of each, marked respectively R and C. The recitative has no regular time, therefore the time mark is 𝄻. The cadence is to be sung in strict 2-4 time, and rapidly. The commas in the words are to be observed, and are accompanied by rests in the music. The syllables in italics are to be prolonged, as indicated by the notes set to them. Let the choir sing this repeatedly, until it is learned.

Then call attention to the fact that the recitative, being all on the same pitch in each of the four parts, is usually—indeed, always—written as one note, the words being adapted to that one note as indicated in this music. Turn to the same chant in Hutchins', No. 319, and call attention to its being the same music. Point out that the words will be found at the end of the *Benedic*, on the opposite page, and show how they are to be adapted to the music in its chant form. Finally, take the first two verses of the *Benedic,* adapt them to the music, and sing them. Then try a *Venite,* say to chant No. 15, singing the *Gloria Patri* first. Always use the *Gloria Patri* in learning new chants. At first, all chants should be single; the double ones will easily follow, in good time.

This method of teaching the chant will be found to be the most practical one that can be used for adult choirs in this country, whether chorus or quartette; our American adult singers are accustomed to rhythmic music only, save one here and there who has had instruction and a little training in the recitative of opera or oratorio music, perhaps in "Vaccai;" and to such this method of writing the chant will convey more real knowledge on the subject than anything else.

The constant tendency in chanting is to "gabble" the recitative, and "drag" the cadence. Insist upon the recitative being sung deliberately, and the cadences rapidly.

It should be well understood, not only by members of the choir, but by all persons in the parish, that *no one* is to be invited to sing with the choir, either occasionally or regularly, save by the clergyman, or the person to whom he may delegate that privilege and authority. Trouble often arises from individual members of the choir asking their musical friends to "come and sing with us," and I have even known wardens and vestrymen to ask strangers to sing with a well-trained vested choir and with no practice whatever with them, without consulting the proper authority.

One trouble, which is usually not long in making its appearance, is irregularity of attendance at practice, and sometimes at service. This should not go unchecked. In a large chorus we must look for some unavoidable irregularity and unpunctuality from serious causes, but the choir must be impressed with the idea that it is best to be regular in punctual attendance. If the choir is so directed and instructed that improvement in singing is manifest to all, it is possible to make much of that fact. Choir singers, in that case, should be given to understand, in plain language, that they receive much more than they give: that the instructions given them in sacred music are valuable—to say nothing of the high honor and privilege of leading in the common praise of the Church. If the members of the choir once become imbued with this idea, however slightly, this one trouble can be met in such a manner as to reduce it to its least dimensions. A polite intimation to a member of the choir that the choice must speedily be made between greater regularity and dismissal becomes a possibility.

The following incidents contain valuable points in this connection. On one occasion a heavy rain had fallen, but by time for practice it had ceased raining. The rector went over to the church to meet the choir, but no one was there. Some ten or fifteen minutes after the hour appointed, two of the men made their appearance, and asked if the practice had been given up. The rector replied that, if such were the case, he was not aware of it. By a little judicious talk, he soon had them quite anxious for a practice. Then he assigned to each of them the task of going out after the missing ones, himself taking the greater number, and in half an hour the choir was ready for practice, and had learned that in their rector's opinion, if in no other, the music of the Church was no trivial affair, to be set aside or neglected for anything which would not cause the neglect of any other work.

In the other case, it was the last practice of the Christmas music, and the principal soprano, a young lady, was absent. Inquiry brought out the fact that she had gone to a party. The rector proceeded to the house

where the party was being given, and having requested to
see the young lady, reminded her that this was the final
practice for the Christmas music, and told her that if she
were not present, she could not sing on Christmas; and
furthermore, that if they could not depend on her for
Christmas, she must cease to consider herself a member of
the choir.   After a moment's thought she recognized the
justice of her rector's demands, excused herself for an
hour, and attended the practice.   But even had she not
done so, and had been dismissed from the choir, it would
have been salutary rather than injurious to the choir,
even though she were the best singer there.

No special rule can be given in such cases; they are
emergencies, and must be met as such.   But an education
in the principles laid down in this chapter will make it
easier to meet them when they arise.

CHAPTER VI.

One occasionally hears a choir whose singing would be very acceptable, if it were not for one or two voices whose very unpleasant peculiarities make them prominent, and render the music disagreeable. Some clergyman will, perhaps, recognize his own choir in these words, and will, involuntarily, think of some one singer whose absence from the choir is an improvement to the music; perhaps it is a bass singer whose musical efforts, to quote the homely expression of a certain bucolic critic of my acquaintance, "sounds like tearin' a rag"—that peculiar grating, rasping, guttural tone which some people adopt to make their voices heard, and in which they certainly succeed beyond their most sanguine expectations. The same effort on the part of a soprano produces an effect painfully suggestive of a cat.

Now, while a clergyman may not presume to enter upon the duties of a professional teacher of the voice, he should be able, if he is conducting his own choir, to correct such faults, as well as to teach his choir how to obtain the best results in their singing. Hence the advisability of a few words, at this point, on the training of voices for choir singing.

The choir should be often reminded that the best choir or chorus effect is produced when no individual voice is prominent; then it is comparatively easy to quell unpleasant voices. Such a voice as I have described can be pleasantly modified and subdued by developing the tone *deep in the throat*, and without any strong effort. "Sing *easily;* don't try to sing loud. Your voice is quite a prominent one, and will be distinctly heard if you sing with a fourth of the power you now use," is what I have often said to such persons.

  You will, of course, have your practising, or some of it, in the church building, where your services are held. You must, occasionally, hear your choir from a distance, as others hear them. Ask them to sing a hymn or chant, and put the length of the church between you and them as they sing it. Watch closely for the *unpleasant* prominent voices; those that are pleasantly prominent may be let alone, if not too prominent: they are rare enough to form an exception to the rule.

The best chorus effect in the soprano is to be obtained by carrying the middle register of the voice (the essential feminine vocal characteristic) as low as D or C sharp below the staff, never allowing the chest tones to rise above those notes. One good authority on this subject says, "Never extend lower registers upward, but strengthen the upper registers and carry them downward, thus equalizing the voices from top to bottom, and enabling your

pupils to sing without straining."* For this purpose the
following exercise may be used :

ah, ah, ah, ah, ah, ah.

The first or second note, probably both, will be sung
easily and with a clear tone. Let all the others be sung
with the same quality of voice, making each tone like the
one preceding it. This can be done by singing them as
marked, diminishing in power. If the lower notes are
sung loud, the tendency in an untrained voice is to use
the chest tone. After this exercise is sung several times,
and the attention of the singers called to the quality of
tone desired, try the following:

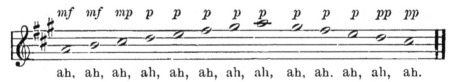

ah, ah, ah, ah, ah, ah, ah, ah, ah, ah. ah, ah, ah.

Impress upon the sopranos that all tones above E
[fifth note in above exercise] should be sung softly, and
thus avoid shrieking. In the descending portion of this
exercise, which is really the important part, persist in the
practice until a clear, flute-like tone is produced. The
proper tone in both exercises can only be produced softly at
first; constant practice will strengthen it. These exercises must be sung by all the sopranos together, although

* Behnke's "Mechanism of the Human Voice."

it is well to try each voice separately on them two or three times. The ladies can be gathered together a half-hour before practice for this work.

Altos are always tempted to carry their chest tones too high. The first exercise just given will be found as useful for them as for the sopranos; and for the cultivation of the upper tones, and the extension of the middle register, the following will be of use:

If any of the alto voices cannot reach the first note— though all should be able to do so—they may begin with the third, or with the second measure. The altos must bear in mind that their part must not be as prominent as the soprano, and in all parts, marked individuality must be discouraged in chorus singing. Endeavor to foster a true *esprit de corps* rather than a personal pride in singing: let all your aim and instruction be "the singing *of the choir*," and not the singing *in* the choir.

As a rule, train your tenors and basses individually rather than collectively. Notice that I say "as a rule," for there are cases once in a while where collective training may be used. Notice what voices among the men are unpleasant or disagreeable in any regard, and when you find such a voice, arrange to meet the possessor of it alone. Then try his voice on the scale over and over again, *forte* and *piano, fortissimo* and *pianissimo,* until you discover and locate a note that he sings pleasingly and properly. Then repeatedly practice that one note, softly at first. until he learns to recognize it himself and understands just how he produces it.   Then take the next note above or below and try to make it resemble that note in quality and power, and in course of time carry out the same idea throughout the entire compass of his voice.

Musically speaking, beware of the "shrieking" soprano, the "bellowing" alto, the "shouting" tenor and the "barking" bass : they are kindred abominations, and the last named evidently models his singing on the E flat tuba of a brass band, as played by the average amateur.   A *persistent* practice of sustained tones sung softly will work surprising effects in all these cases.

"Husky" voices are often benefitted by steady practice of what is sometimes called the "stroke" or "shock" of the glottis ; also by repeated endeavors to sing loud tones with the least possible amount of breath, being directed to "sing the tone long and loud, and *hold back the breath.*"

Nasal voices have no place in the choir.   If they are there, however, and you can not see your way clear to banishing them, constantly impress upon them that *pianissimo* music is their *forte.*

If the work set forth in this chapter is carried out, even to a moderate degree, its effect will be found in uniting the choir in tone, which will lead to union in sentiment and endeavor.   Every member will

perceive and appreciate the point that he is receiving
material benefit from his connection with the choir—that
the instruction alone fully repays him for what trouble
he may take to attend practices and services.

These exercises should be often repeated, especially as
new singers enter; and doubtless other work of this
nature will suggest itself. As the choir progresses in its
singing, a higher class of music may be used, and occasionally a good anthem or setting of the TE DEUM, or the
evening canticles may be prepared for special service.
But the choir should never for an instant be allowed to
lose sight of its true standing and office—that of leading
the congregation in the singing of *G*od's praise.

CHAPTER VII.

THE QUARTETTE CHOIR.

The mixed quartette choir is by no means to be ignored or despised. It is common, now-a-days, to speak of it contemptuously and slightingly, in some quarters even bitterly, to call it "unchurchly," and to refer to it as an "abomination," an "unmitigated evil," all of which is unfair and unjust. There may be some quartette choirs that merit such stinging and harsh words, but—there are quartette choirs and quartette choirs.

But, it must be acknowledged that the quartette choir is more likely to act upon mistaken ideas, and has stronger temptation to become unchurchly in its music and methods than any other form of choir. With but one voice to each part, and that usually a voice of more than ordinary ability and culture, this choir feels it to be a waste of time and talent if no music is attempted of a more elaborate nature than is possible for a chorus to sing. The musical taste is continually tempted to overwhelm the devotional sense ; or in some instances, perhaps, that music which appeals to and expresses the devotional sense of the trained soloist is to the ordinary ear only the display of the concert room.

If such cultured singers will but study—as they well know how—the music of the Church, and become thoroughly imbued with its spirit, they will value and appreciate it as no other choirs can. But, unfortunately, there is a prejudice to overcome, in most cases. Such music, they suppose is impossible to them, and can only be rendered by a chorus, and they are not chorus singers, but soloists. I speak on these points from repeated experience as a member of such choirs, in various capacities.

There is a method of minimizing this disadvantage; briefly stated, it is this: Each member of the quartette should be engaged in two capacities—first, as a soloist; second as one trained in *technique,* expression and power, *to lead the congregation in song.* All hymns must be sung from a certain specified hymnal, and the tune must invariably be that to which the words are set in that hymnal, the simplest or best known being used where a choice of tunes is given. About once a month, let the first half-hour of a practice be devoted to new hymn tunes and chants, when the congregation may be invited to attend and join in the practice. All hymns must be canonically selected, *i. e.,* by the clergyman. The *Venite* and all glorias [including the *Gloria Tibi* and—generally—the *Gloria in Excelsis*] must be sung to easy chants selected from the hymnal, as should also be one of the canticles of Evening Prayer, save on the greater festivals, when only the glorias in the psalter and one hymn need be congregational, and "Praise *G*od from Whom all blessings flow," sung to "Old Hundred" at the Presentation of Alms. This is not impracticable. It was strictly carried out in one quartette of which I was the organist. At first it seemed the height of absurdity to sing one of Thomas' or Millard's *Jubilates*, and at its close to modulate to the proper key and sing a Gregorian or Anglican chant to the *Gloria*, instead of the author's music. But the grand effect of the congregational unison is sufficient to disarm prejudice on that score; it is something which might often be done with great satisfaction by any choir—even a vested one.

There is under such an arrangement abundant opportunity for the choir to sing that style of music to which it is peculiarly adapted—in other words, to fulfil their engagement as soloists. The service may be preceded by an anthem, during which the clergyman enters; a solo, duo, trio or quartette may be sung during the collection of the offerings; there is also a special place in Evening Prayer for an anthem, and another anthem, or elaborate hymn setting, can be sung after the Benediction, during which the clergyman retires. Occasionally, or even usually, an anthem setting of a Te Deum, or one of the Evening Canticles, might be used. Care should be taken to avoid the use of adaptations of certain compositions whose general associations are far from churchly, such as operatic airs or well-known German songs.

Sometimes a clergyman, especially in a new field, finds a paucity of available singers, but is able to get together

a quartette of fairly good voices. In such a case, it is wise
to use them.   First, he must train them in singing metrical hymns in strict time and with even power.   Leading
a congregation in song does not admit of any very fine
shading in *pp* and *rallentando*, still less in *accellerando* and
a piacere singing.   Then should follow training in the
chants, as outlined in chapter V.

No chant for congregational use led by a quartette
should run above F in the treble; E flat is a safer limit,
and a necessary one in unisons.   The Quartette will find
it useful, even in the commonest Anglican chants, to sing
occasional verses in unison, or, in some of the longer
chants, to sing in antiphon unisons, the female and male
voices alternating.   For example, the *Venite* may be sung
by a congregation led by a quartette choir with excellent
effect, the choir singing in this manner:

First verse, full unison;   verses 2, 3 and **4**, full
harmony; verse 5, female voices in unison; verse **6**, male
voices in unison; verse 7, female voices in unison; verse
8, male voices in unison; verse 9, full harmony; *Gloria,*
full unison [or, verse 7, full harmony; verse 8, full unison.
Other variations in the different chants will occur to the
thoughtful and judicious director.

It is not difficult to imagine circumstances under
which the quartette is the only choir available.   But in
its formation the same ideas should prevail that are set
forth in the preceding pages; the choir must understand
that there is canonical authority over them in the matter

of music, and that their position is chiefly to lead the congregation in singing. If singers seeking, or desiring, or willing to accept positions in quartette choirs are not willing to sing under these churchly restrictions, do not engage them, no matter how talented and accomplished they may be, or how high their standing in the musical world; they are lacking in certain very essential qualities —among which is common sense—if they can not under- stand the Church's right to regulate and direct the musical portion of her services equally with the ritual, or, under- standing it, are not willing to submit to it.

There is another form of choir, having points in common with both the quartette and the mixed chorus, namely, the double quartette, composed of eight voices,* two voices on each of the four parts, instead of one. Almost all that has been said in this chapter is applicable to this form of choir, as well as many things in the chapters on the Mixed Choir.

One thing which is possible to this choir is antiphonal quartette singing, as well as the method of antiphon unison; and with proper care in forming it, a quartette of female voices and one of male voices may be secured, which will give a most agreeable variety in Offertory music, anthems, etc., and a greater volume of tone is secured for leading the congregation.

---

* Eight voices do not necessarily constitute a double quartette; there must be two voices on each part. Any variation from this would consti- tute a chorus choir.

The combination of quartette and mixed choir is not an uncommon one, and has much to recommend it. The chorus gives the power needed, while the trained voices are left more at liberty for their own specialties; and certain choruses with obligato movements, such as the *Inflammatus,* in the *Stabat Mater,* can be prepared and presented with proper effect.

CHAPTER VIII.

The careless and faulty pronunciation of many singers is notorious. Good choir singing requires more than correct intonation and good volume of tone; it requires the words to be correctly pronounced, and rendered in such a manner that they may be distinctly understood without a book in the hand of the hearer to follow them. I remember several years ago reading an item that went the rounds of the press, indicating the manner in which some choir rendered the hymn beginning:

"Welcome, sweet day of rest."

The effect of these words as sung by this choir, was

"Waw kaw swaw daw aw raw,

and so on throughout the hymn.

Given a church building with an echo, and this illustration is hardly exaggerated. Mr. Stubbs, in his little book, "Practical Hints on Boy Choir Training"—a book which ought to be in the hands of every director of a vested choir—in a foot-note on p. 65, says: "The author once heard a choir of considerable reputation sing Barnby's anthem 'Break forth,' etc., thus—'Break farth into jy, break farth into jy, sing tuggether ye waste places zof Jeerusalum !' The same choir sang vociferously in another anthem, 'Hosanner in the highest, Hosanner in the highest !' " I distinctly remember once hearing a choir sing a hymn of which I could not catch one single word until during the third stanza, when I gathered enough to assure me they were attempting the familiar hymn beginning, "Now from the altar of our hearts."

There are a few words which, in spite of the *dicta* of certain purists, cannot be pronounced in singing as in speaking, although, as a rule, the same pronunciation should prevail in both speech and song. Such a word is "pardon," the pronunciation of which Webster gives as "par-dn." Now as, in singing, the length of the note must be given to the vowel sound, that vowel sound must be given in the second syllable, although it is not to be sounded in speaking.

The following three general principles should govern every singer in pronunciation :

1. Give all vowels and consonants their proper sounds.

2. Never disconnect syllables or words that ought to be kept together.

3. Never join words together that ought to be kept apart.

The following rules, based on these three principles, will be found very useful in choir work :

1. Such words as pass, last, path, rather, after, should have, in singing, the pure Italian sound of a—*ah:* e. g., pahss, lahst, pahth, rahther, ahfter.

Caution : (a.) Do not give this sound in words where it does not properly belong, as, e. g., hand, land. (b.) Never insert an *r*, and say parse, larst, parth, etc.

Special words : Abraham should be pronounced "Ah-brah-hahm ;" Israel, when in three syllables, "Is-rah-el ;" be careful, in this word, not to say "Is-rah-*yell*," as I have heard it sung. Jehovah—first syllable should have the short sound of e ; "Jeh-ho-vah," not "Jee-ho-var ;" Jerusalem should be pronounced in the same way—"Jeh-ru-sah-lem," not "Jee-roo-say-lem."

2. Words ending with *ain* unaccented, should have nearly the same sound as if accented, in singing, namely, the short sound of *e*, as in "again": e. g., mountain pronounced "mounten ;" bargain, pronounced "bargen."

• 3. Pronounce properly the short sounds of all vowels, even if unaccented, and never replace the sound of one vowel with that belonging to another. e. g., Vanity often mispronounced "vanutty ;" worship, "worshup ;"* Creator, "Creater."

4. As the tone maintains its length on the vowel element in a word or syllable, it is necessary to sound all consonants clearly and distinctly, almost explosively.

5. In compound vowel sounds, give the length to the *principle*, not to the "vanishing" element: e. g. The word "light ;" the long sound of i is a compound, composed of

---

* In connection with this word, so commonly mispronounced, I have sometimes reminded my choir that a merchant never *shups* his goods; he *ships* them.

"ah" for the principle, and "ee" for the vanish. Therefore sing the word "lah—eet," and not "lace—t."

These five rules are based on the first of the three principles above set forth. On the second principle we may build the following:

Never pause or breathe between the syllables of a word. e. g., The line, "Life is a shadow, how it flies," sung to the tune "Hebron," with this effect: "Life is a shad, oh how it flies."

Exception: In such compositions as "Mighty Jehovah," by Bellini (not very Churchly music, by the way, but useful for illustration in this place) we find it necessary to pause between the syllables of words to secure a *musical* effect which is here allowed to predominate.

And the third principle gives rise to the following important rules:

1. Avoid running words together in such a manner as to produce a sound connecting the two which is foreign to either. e. g., Praise ye, bless ye, that ye, often sung, prazhee, bleshee, thatchee: such words should, if necessary, have a decided pause between them.

2. Avoid running words together in such a manner as to alter the sense. e. g., Hymn 5, Church Hymnal, third stanza; the next to the last line is almost invariably sung, "A pup, ye heirs of glory," instead of "Up, up, ye heirs" etc.

Illustration: A choir unobservant of this rule once

sang the words, "The consecrated cross I'd bear," with such startling effect that a little child afterward asked his parents what sort of an animal a "consecrated cross-eyed bear" was, that they sang about in church. A very slight pause after the word "cross," would have remedied this.

3. In words of two or more syllables having the last syllable *un*accented, sing that last syllable lightly, as it is usually pronounced in speaking.

Note: This rule well followed, is invaluable in compound time as well as in chanting, both in recitative and cadence.

4. Never pause or breathe *after* an unimportant word; if necessary, take the breath just before it.

5. Observe marks of punctuation and rhetorical pauses.

Example illustrating both of these rules : The chorus "And the glory of the Lord," from the oratorio of the Messiah, usually rendered, "And the glory the,—glory of the Lord."

As to such words as either, neither, wound, wind, and all words that have two pronunciations, the best rule for a choir is to follow the pronunciation of the minister.

Let me add here a few words on the subject of expression. Due attention to the words ought to indicate to any ordinary intellect whether the tone should be loud or soft. The hymn, "Father, whate'er of earthly bliss," should not be sung with as much power as, "All hail the power of Jesus' name;" every member of a choir should possess sufficient intelligence to know this. Some hymnals have the expression marks for everything to be sung, which is a great saving of time to the director, and a very beneficial thing, if the marking is done intelligently.

Choirs sometimes need practical training on the basis that *piano* does not mean *lento*, and that *diminuendo* is not necessarily to be associated with *rallentando*. A good way to correct this common fault, I have found, is to have the choir often sing an entire tune *very softly and rapidly*.

CHAPTER IX.

GENERAL.

Choir Facilities and Properties—The place for the choir in church—the organ and the organist.

CHOIR FACILITIES AND PROPERTIES.

In every church building where it can be done, a special room should be furnished for the use of the choir, which room could, of course, be used for other purposes when not in use by them. It should be furnished with a piano or cabinet organ for use in practicing, and should contain certain shelf-closets, or cases, furnished with lock and key, for the safe keeping of hymnals, sheet and manuscript music, extra prayer books, and other things that a choir might find useful or convenient. It would also furnish a convenient place for the disposal of heavy wraps and overcoats in winter, umbrellas and rubbers in rainy weather, as well as a place to gather for final hints as to the music, just before service.

In pleasant weather, most choirs prefer to practice in the church, with the accompaniment of the church organ; but in the winter this necessitates the heating of the building, and other accompanying inconveniences.

Of course, in a small church building such a room would probably be an impossibility. I have frequently, in such case, when not best to use the church, held choir practice at some private residence.

THE PLACE FOR THE CHOIR IN THE CHURCH.

The obsolescent custom of putting the choir in an elevated gallery at the rear of the church is a most absurd one. The proper place for the leaders of the people in singing is in front of them, where they can be seen and distinctly heard without any change of attitude on the part of the people. An elevated place in front and to one side, near the chancel, is the proper place for any choir— except a vested one. The singers should never face the congregation, but stand sidewise; and in churches where the priest assumes the "eastward position," it is needless to say, the choir should also do so, turning to the altar at all Glorias, Creeds and Gospels.

THE ORGAN AND THE ORGANIST.

The best instrument for use in church is, of course,. the pipe organ. Regarding this instrument it is not necessary to write at length, as any parish possessing the means to procure such an instrument, also possesses the means, pecuniary and otherwise, of obtaining all necessary information in regard to it.

In smaller or weaker parishes that are not able to.

indulge in such an outlay as will secure a *good* pipe organ —for a poor one is an abomination—the "Vocalion" is an admirable substitute. But there are many parishes—indeed, they are largely in the majority—that are unable to bear even this much expense. In such churches, a good cabinet organ will answer every purpose. A little advice to such parishes is not amiss here, and indeed is often sorely needed.

Do, not, under any circumstances, buy a *cheap* instrument. The mails are flooded with circulars to clergymen offering cabinet organs at a less price than a good instrument can possibly be made for; and sensible people who would never buy a watch or a sewing-machine, or even a shotgun so advertised, will depart from their principles when it comes to the purchase of a musical instrument, especially if it is for church use.

It is always safe to buy a *new* Burdette or Estey organ; there are a few other makers whose instruments are sure to be good, but it is not possible to name them all here. The advice of some honest and competent music teacher, *who would not be likely to have a personal interest in the sale,* would prove useful on this point. Occasionally, one is fortunate enough to find an instrument of inferior make that turns out good, but to buy such instruments, as also to buy second handed ones, is a risk.

Regarding organists, advice—as in the case of organs—is not so necessary for large parishes as for small ones. Any person who can handle a large church organ with sufficient skill to secure an engagement as organist, generally possesses sufficient taste, judgment, and other needed qualifications, either naturally or by acquisition, to successfully perform the functions demanded. It is in the small parish where the greatest difficulties are to be encountered in this regard.

The cabinet organ may be played in such a manner as to materially aid the singing, or it may be so handled as to be a hindrance. If the player is inexperienced, it is well to select all tunes a full week in advance, that the organist may have sufficient practice in them to play them smoothly, correctly, and without hesitation. Church attendants in large cities do not realize the trials of many small country parishes in this regard. The following actual experience may be something new to them, and may convey a useful hint to some clergyman.

I once undertook to conduct services for a while on Sunday afternoons in a little country church which stood all alone out on the prairie. The organist was a young girl, who also led the singing with a whoop and a shriek. She was a very inexperienced player, and I was very kindly cautioned about her peculiar methods, just before service began, by one of the vestrymen, a worthy stock-farmer, whose idioms were all of a "horsy" character.

"The girl that plays the organ," he explained, "is a young creature, but perfectly good-natured and gentle; I don't know enough about music myself to judge of her merits very well, but it's very evident that she occasionally shies at an unexpected sharp or flat; and, another thing, if she comes to any obstruction in the tune that she balks at, she just trots back to the starting-ropes and tries it over again; we all humor her on that point, and somehow or other, we generally manage to pull through. I just thought I'd mention this," he concluded, "because a person always likes to know what to expect; I know *I* do if I get hold of a strange *horse*, and I suppose a minister is the same when he gets into a strange *church*."

The service proceeded very smoothly; the chants were sung with no breaks, although the tone was rather crude, and the cadences were sung exceedingly slow; but the evident hearty enjoyment of the people in the singing was the best kind of music in itself. But the first hymn contained an "obstruction," although I had purposely selected a familiar and easy tune, "Federal Street," Hymn 387. The "young creature" sounded the first chord, and started off in the lead in very good style, with the congregation after: "Stay, Thou long-suf—" *(mistake:* B *natural instead of flat, in the air).* She stopped short, and so did the people. They "humored her," as my informant put it; and all begun again: "Stay, Thou long suf—" *(same mistake).* All the congregation very obligingly, and in a perfectly matter-of-course way, began again, and this time it went through triumphantly with no further mishaps; but it took the entire time occupied by the singing of the hymn for me to recover myself sufficiently to proceed with the service, and I did not dare venture on the announcement of the other hymn. Before leaving the church, I selected the hymns for the next Sunday afternoon, and requested the organist to practice them during the intervening week. At the next service I led the hymns myself, and disregarded all breaks and "balks," if there were any, on the part of the "young creature" at the organ.

By careful attention and practice, the young amateur can learn the ways of the service, and can acquire all the necessary skill in accompanying the singing with the cabinet organ. In a small parish it is advisable to have three or four organists in training from among the young people, allowing first one, then another, to play in Sunday School and at week-day services, thus "breaking them in" for future work in connection with the choir. This is a plan which I have always adopted, and I have found it to work admirably.

CHAPTER X.

*Special Choirs—School Choirs—Children's Music—
Festal Music.*

SPECIAL CHOIRS.

For a parochial mission, a Good Friday "Three Hours,"
or some other special service, it is sometimes advisable—
even necessary—to form a choir to sing on that occasion
only, as perhaps the members of the regular choir are
unable to attend, or a larger choir is desired.

In forming such a choir, the "hap-hazard" method is
as much to be deprecated as it is in forming the regular
choir. It is better, first, before taking any active steps, to
decide how large a choir is desirable, and how it must be
proportioned in the four parts, and other things that the
occasion may demand. Then, ascertain upon how many
members of the regular choir you can depend. When
this is clearly settled, and you know just what you want,
invite outsiders as you think best, either by public invita-
tion, or personally, or both.

The practice of such a choir should be closely confined
to the music of the service or services for which it is

organized. The finer details of expression, phrasing, etc., which may occupy considerable time and study in the regular choir, must, of necessity, be omitted, or only casually touched upon. The general effect is all that is possible. If the choir is organized for a parochial mission, the soprano should largely predominate ; and as the music for mission use is all of the simplest description, good volume, strict time, clear enunciation, and correct pronunciation of words are all that can be labored for.

SCHOOL CHOIRS.

In our schools we have peculiar conditions for the formation of choirs. In a boys' school, a full vested choir is among the possibilities, as some of the older boys or of the teachers may sing tenor and bass, or those parts can be filled, to some extent, by men residing near by, who are not otherwise connected with the school. But in a girls' school we have, at the most, only two kinds of voices, soprano and alto. Still, if there are one or two high sopranos and an equal number of deep contraltos among them, good four-part harmony can be produced for occasions. The same limitation applies to our Theological schools, with the difference that all the voices are male. With one or two high tenors and the same number of deep basses, four-part harmony is also possible.

Unison services will be found the best adapted, in a general way, to such conditions, and Gregorian tones may be freely used. But as this book is concerned with *parish* choirs, these are matters that must be left to specialists and experts.

CHILDREN'S MUSIC.

The singing of the Sunday School is of the nature of congregational singing; but it must be borne in mind that children, by the very nature of childhood, demand lively, fresh, stirring *melodies*. It is difficult in attempting to avoid the Scylla of the over-rich (for children) harmonies of the music of the Church, to keep from running on to the Charybdis of the popular gigatic* Sunday School music of the present day. It is devoutly to be hoped that some good composer will be raised up, with the love of God and little children so filling his entire being that he will not fear, or care for, would-be classical critics, and will, consequently, write such music for children as their nature craves, and the great need of the Church in this matter demands.

We already have a little of such music; and if all our books of children's music could be gathered together, and a selection made from them of such pieces as are suitable

---

* *Gigatic.* The use of this word may seem to some purists to demand justification, which is here given: In the review of a certain new book of alleged Sunday School music, in a prominent sectarian paper, this word makes its *debut* as follows: "It must be conceded that in this large collection of Sabbath School music, Mr. —— has undertaken and successfully completed a most gigatic work." At first, we regarded the word ' gigatic" as a typographical error, supposing the reviewer had written it "gigantic;" but a casual examination of the book under review satisfied us that the intelligent compositor was all right–he had followed copy. From the very nature of the case, the reviewer had seen the necessity— and acted upon it—of adding a new and much needed word to our vocabulary, freshly coined from the Italian *gig ι,* a jig.

for children—the judgment of the little ones themselves being consulted—we might possibly have one excellent collection, if not a very large one, of good music for our children.

Children should early be taught how to chant properly, singing the recitative with due deliberation, and the cadences rapidly and heartily. I have invariably found children particularly partial to some of the Gregorian tones, as the *Tonus Regius,* the *Rouen Mediation* (v, 5), Tone iii, 4, and one or two others, after they have become somewhat familiar with them; and they arrive, in course of time, to an appreciation of good music, and of classical (if not too elaborate) harmonies.

FESTAL MUSIC.

On festal occasions, when the heart is filled with emotions of joy and gratitude to God, it is very seemly and appropriate that our music should correspond, and it is not at all unbecoming to carefully prepare and offer to God, at such a time, our very best endeavors—in music, as in other offerings.

The feeling underlying all this is a natural one, implanted in our beings by God Himself; it manifests itself in various ways, and is to be commended as long as the outward manifestations of that feeling do not usurp the place of true worship, and as long as we bear in mind that there is not only a *feeling* to be considered and manifested, but a *principle* as well.

Both principle and feeling impel us to make careful preparation for such occasions, not only that we may indicate our sense and appreciation of the value and importance of that which the service is designed to commemorate, but also that we may render unto God a service which has cost us in its preparation some labor, and perhaps—more pleasing in His sight—some self-denial. We even take extra pains with our own personal appearance, which is praiseworthy if it be, as it should, from a desire to offer God even that personal appearance at its best. In our offerings of our means in the Offertory, the same principle should actuate us, namely, the offering of the fruits of careful, painstaking preparation in the way of labor or self-denial. So with our music. But if the underlying motive is pride, in all or any of these things, not only is it apt to be overdone, but the offering itself is a "vain oblation."

Care must be taken in our music, as in everything else, not to attempt what is beyond our ability. The choir must bear this in mind in its preparation, and not try to render music of which it is not capable. For a choir whose capacity is only equal to the simple chants and metrical tunes of the ordinary Sunday services to attempt, say, on Easter, Eyre's setting to the Communion Office, or one of Stainer's, Smart's or Buck's heaviest *Te Deums,* would be more than absurd, it would be wrong.

And choirs that are capable of this heavy work should reserve such music for festal occasions, and by no means

use it constantly, as it is beyond the appreciation of the
average congregation, and is, therefore, no incentive or
aid to devotion.

Again, in the preparation of festal music, it must be
borne in mind that the people must not be deprived of the
right and privilege of joining their voices with those of
the choir in some ascriptions of praise, and the endeavor
should be to see *how much* hearty congregational singing
is possible, consistent with the special festal music of the
choir, not, as is too often the case, *how little*. Such hymn
tunes as Hebron, Coronation, Duke Street, Arlington,
Balerma, Mear, Worgan, Adeste Fideles, can be selected
for the hymns, and the festal atmosphere of the occasion
be thereby more pronounced, as well as better appreciated
and enjoyed.

CHAPTER XI

Forming the Choir—Its Organization—Vestments.

The vested choir of men and boys is the distinctively
churchly choir. It is an organization *sui generis*, and
requires more care, attention and practice, as well as more
rigid discipline, than any other form of choir. It is
available in almost every parish, however small, although
not always expedient. As to its availability, I know of a
very small parish where the rector spent the first two
years of his incumbency in vainly trying to form a mixed
choir, or even—what he supposed to be his only possible
choice,—a quartette. At last, in sheer desperation, he
began to look about for boys ; to his surprise and delight
he soon had a choir of ten boys and six men in training,
and could have had more. It was crude material, all of
it, but in the course of a year he had a choir capable of
rendering the music of the service in a very acceptable
manner.

Several things are essential to success, not only in the
formation, but also in the continuance of such a choir.
If you are in hearty sympathy with boys, really like to be

with them, can enter with honest pleasure into the enjoyment of their plans and games (if not into the games
themselves), and know yourself to be possessed of the
power of governing them, you can make such a choir a
success. Otherwise, if you desire such a choir, you should
procure some trustworthy man, who possesses these
needful qualifications, as your choirmaster.

This choir demands great care and labor from the
nature of the boy's voice, as well as the nature of the boy
himself. The attention required to be paid to the men
and their voices is very little more than is required in an
ordinary mixed choir with good musical aspirations. The
most of the time and care must be expended on the boys;
and their voices are not permanent; at the age of puberty
the boy's voice changes more or less gradually to the
man's, and during this period his voice is absolutely
useless, and his place in the choir must be filled. From
the nature of the material of this choir, this is a very
serious matter.

In any other choir, if a singer drops out, all that is
necessary is to secure another. But when a boy ceases
to sing, not only must another boy be found to fill his
place, but all the work which was done in training the
old chorister must be repeated with the new boy. Thus
a vested choir is a scene of unending vocal training—not
to higher and still higher points, however, but the same
thing over and over again—a sort of treadmill. And
then, too, it is necessary to have some hold on the boy

after the gloss of novelty has worn off; boys must be kept interested. More new music must be used than in other choirs, which is a considerable item of expense, to say nothing of medals, prizes, treats, etc., which are very precious in the sight of the average boy.

But the advantages and superiority of a *good* choir of this nature, fully compensate for all these drawbacks. The vigor and freshness of boys' voices have an inspiriting effect on the singing of the men, and the music possesses a force and *verve* unattainable to any other choir. Both men and boys begin, in due time, to acquire an interest in the Church, apart from the music. An objector to vested choirs once said to me, in a carping and fault-finding spirit, "There is no knowing where it will end." And truly there is no knowing. I have heard that, in one instance, it ended in a choir-boy eventually becoming a Bishop!

The *esprit de corps* in such a choir is very marked, and the men and boys become very strongly attached to each other. If the men are frequently reminded of the influence of their lives and conduct on the boys, it gives a strong inducement to the higher life. And the matter of influence is not confined to the men alone. More than one community has reaped signal benefit from the influence of a vested choir, without realizing to what they were indebted for the manifest improvement in the manners and morals of the boys generally. If the boys of the choir are taught that their daily lives must correspond with their position in the Church, the attempt to lead such a life cannot fail to have its influence upon other boys with whom they associate at school or play.

The first necessity in forming a choir of this kind is to clearly ascertain how large a choir is desired. The size of the choir should be in proportion to the size of the church building, as a general rule. A choir of eight voices is large enough for some churches, while others could use ten times that number. After this point is decided, then the proportions—*i. e.,* the number of voices desired on each of the four parts in the harmony—must be considered and determined. The best musical effects will generally be produced where the sopranos equal in number all the other singers, as in the following tables:

CHOIR OF EIGHT.

Sopranos 4   Alto 1   Tenor 1   Basses 2

CHOIR OF TWELVE.

Sopranos 6   Altos 2   Tenor 1 (or 2)   Basses 3 (or 2)

CHOIR OF TWENTY.

Sopranos 10   Altos 4   Tenors 2   Basses 4

CHOIR OF TWENTY-SIX.

Sopranos 12   Altos 4   Tenors 4   Basses 6

In choirs of twenty and above, it is better to have even numbers in all the parts, for convenience in the division of the choir into two equal parts. Hence in the above table, the number of sopranos is 12 instead of 13.

CHOIR OF THIRTY.

Sopranos 16 (or 14)　　Altos 4 (or 6)　　Tenors 4　　Basses 6

CHOIR OF FORTY.

Sopranos 20　　Altos 6 (or 8) Tenors 6 (or 4)　　Basses 8

CHOIR OF FIFTY.

Sopranos 24　　Altos 8 (or 6)　　Tenors 6 (or 8)　　Basses 12

This, however, is not a "law of the Medes and Persians." Voices differ in power to such an extent that this proportion must oftentimes be varied—it may be, greatly so. Thus, one of the best choirs I ever heard contained thirty-eight voices, proportioned as follows:

Sopranos 12　　Altos 8　　Tenors 8　　Basses 10.

The sopranos in this choir possessed remarkably powerful voices, while the other singers were by no means robust in tone, but made up a good volume by their number.

Having decided upon the size of the choir and its proportions in the various parts—subject, of course, to change, dependent on the relative strength of the voices secured—let it be publicly known that you desire to procure choristers between the ages of nine and fifteen, so many boys for soprano, so many for alto; also give the probable number of tenors and basses needed. Specify a time for meeting boys to try their voices and to select from them the number you require. Ask your teachers of boys' classes in the Sunday School to talk it over with their boys, and to aid in creating enthusiasm on the subject. You will need to use personal work and influence to secure the attendance of some of the men, but a few once secured, these will usually bring in others.

When you meet the boys, as above directed, to try their voices, first let them sing some familiar tune together; then try the voices individually and separately. Try each boy on the same hymn that all have sung together, then let him vocalize* the scales, beginning with the scale of C, and singing in succession, quite slowly, the scales of D flat, D, E flat, E and F, until you get a fair idea of the quality and range of his voice. Some voices will need a little coaxing and humoring at the very outset to accomplish even this. Some boys, while capable of doing it, absolutely *do not know how* to sound a tone as played on an instrument. With such, the best way is to find on the instrument the tone which they sound with the voice, and from that to lead them gradually—note by note—to the tone desired. Adopt some method of recording each voice as tried, that when you have tried them all you may have a definite knowledge : some such record as the following, will be sufficient : Write down each boy's name, his age, whether baptized or no, and such other points as you desire, and then indicate, by letters—a, b, c, or by numbers, the standing of his voice—say 1, for excellent in tone, quality, compass ; 2, good ; 3, fair ; 4, poor ; 5, rejected.

After all have been tried, form your soprano and alto

---

* To *vocalize* is simply to sing "ah" to each note.

corps, first including all marked 1; if that is not sufficient, add from those marked 2, 3 and 4 successively, of course rejecting all marked 5. If any remain, invite them to come and practice with the choir for a while, as they may be needed.

Very often a rejected voice will, by careful work, come out in good shape. One of the finest high sopranos I ever had in a choir was rejected at first, as having a coarse, disagreeable tone of voice, and being unable to sound a tone as played on the instrument.

Boys under nine years of age are of no use in the choir, and indeed ten is a better limit. They are not good readers, nor are they yet developed enough intellectually. But from that age they are useful, and grow more and more so, until the change of voice, which occurs at the age of 16, sometimes as early as 15, and in some rare instances—more common in the southern latitudes—as early as 14 or 13. As the voice begins to change, we will often find the change to be so gradual that a soprano can be transferred to alto, and sing that part for some time. Some choirmasters, after the first year or so of their choir's existence, keep their alto ranks filled in this manner, and the boys come to regard it as a promotion.

After a sufficient preliminary training, as outlined in chapter XIII, the men may be called on to meet with the boys; any of the men who do not read music should, of course, have some instruction also, during this time; then it is well to *organize* the choir, setting forth disciplinary rules, appointing officers, assigning numbers, and otherwise putting the choir into shape for effective work. If the choir is a large one, and you intend to divide it into *Decani* and *Cantoris*, do not make that division until you become well acquainted with the voices and capabilities of the singers, that the two sides may be as nearly equal as possible.

All *choir* officers should be appointed by the rector, not elected by the choir. The choirmaster may request the rector to formally appoint such officers as he desires, or—what is often a better way—the rector may delegate the choirmaster to make such appointments in his name. The *election* of officers should be confined to such organizations as may be formed within the choir, or in connection therewith, such as the "Choir Club," described in a. subsequent chapter.

The following is a good form of organization : The choir officers to consist of, 1. The rector, who is president of the organization ; 2. The choirmaster, who is warden and director; 3. The organist, whose duties are well understood ; 4. The crucifer, who shall carry the cross in all processions of the choir, and who need not be a singer; 5. The clerk, who shall keep a faithful record of all services and choir rehearsals with the attendance and punctuality of the choir, also, for reference, shall keep a file of programmes of all services ; 6. The librarian, or curator, who shall have charge of all books and music used in the choir (the crucifer may be utilized for this office); 7. The collectors, who shall gather up the offerings of the choir at all services where an offering is made, and reverently place it on the plates or alms-basin; one or two of the little boys will do this work very well.

Such a choir needs long preliminary training before entering upon active duty in the service of the Church; from three to nine months will be required, according to habits, previous musical knowledge, etc., of the singers. The boys should, as before intimated, be trained separately for some time, and all bass and tenor singers who have never sung before, and do not read music, must be put under instruction also. And while this preliminary work is being done, the vestments must be prepared.

The proper vestments for a choir are the cassock and cotta. The first, made of some black goods, should reach nearly to the floor, and the cotta, which should always be of pure linen, should reach about to the knees. The Roman pattern of cassock is the best, being more easily made, containing less cloth, and more readily kept in order than any other—except for the organist, who should wear an Anglican cassock; this being open from the belt to the floor, gives him the free use of his feet on the organ pedals. (Of course, it is understood that if the organist is a lady, she wears no choir vestments).

Some parishes procure their vestments, both choir and clerical, from one of the English houses, or have them made by some large Church guild that advertises to do such work. This is an easy, and usually a satisfactory way. But if the ladies of the parish will form a sewing-society for this especial purpose, and purchase the material and make the vestments themselves, they will experience a sense of satisfaction and appreciation that the same goods purchased ready-made can never furnish.

Good cassock patterns can be procured from the Butterick Company, and cotta patterns can usually be obtained from any parish that has a vested choir; or both patterns can be procured from the guilds mentioned in the preceding paragraph. The Anglican cassock for the organist, however, would probably have to be purchased ready made. All vestments should have a strong loop at the back of the neck-band to hang them up by, also the name of the chorister who wears them, written in indelible ink on a piece of tape or linen, easily detachable, in case the vestment is to be transferred to another, as is often the case among growing boys.

A committee. of ladies should have the care of the vestments, looking them over at regular intervals, to see that there are no rips, that the loops are secure, no cassock buttons missing, and particularly that there is nothing in cassock pockets to attract mice. These little pests seem to be quite fond of Brown's Bronchial Troches, peppermint drops, and the like medicaments, which not only boys, but men, carry into the choir in their cassock pockets, under the supposition that they are effectual aids in singing, but forget to remove them at the close of service. The mice, in their endeavors to get these delicacies, are not particular as to how they get at them, and evidently prefer to gnaw through the outside of the cassock to the coveted dainty. The cottas should go to the ⸴laundry at least once a month, where it should be distinctly understood that *no starch whatever* is to be used on them.

Once or twice a year, the vestments must all be refitted to the boys, as many]will have outgrown theirs. This is not such a difficult or tedious task as one might suppose, as some of the larger boys may have dropped out, and other smaller ones may have been admitted in the meantime. It is a good idea, however, to have two or three extra sets of vestments in the choir.

CHAPTER XII.

Discipline—Rules—Attendance.

A vested choir needs decided and strict discipline. Boys are accustomed to such at school, and they respect, and even admire, a choirmaster who can and does govern them with firmness. The "boy" nature is exceedingly liable to come to the surface, after he becomes familiar with his surroundings, and that nature is usually lacking in reverence. This must be controlled, and the boy must learn and realize that misbehavior in the choir is even a more serious matter than at school. What rules are made should be strictly enforced; it is not wise to have any "dead letter" laws among them.

It is hardly possible to maintain too rigid discipline, although it is possible to be too harsh and "cross" in enforcing it. The choirmaster who can show himself "a boy among boys" at the proper times, is the one who, by determination and will power, can have the best discipline in his choir.' There are choirmasters who are very lax in this regard, from fear that strict discipline will drive boys away from the choir. If they would only draw the reins a little tighter, they would receive a new revelation as the result.

Boys like to be talked to by any one who has something to say, and can say it pleasantly and in a spirited manner. The most unpalatable things will be received in the kindliest way, if they are only presented properly. A thorough idea of what you want to say, and a brief and spirited way of saying it, with—if possible—a fair knowledge of the "boy" vocabulary, will appeal at once to the consciences and good sense of the boys. In trying to impress a needed truth, Scriptural and other illustrations are decidedly in order, and are highly appreciated, if pertinent to the subject. A typical "talk to a choir" is produced in a subsequent chapter.

The best plan to follow in making rules, is to wait till' the occasion arises for them. One or two must be made at once, such as the following:

RULE 1.
Members of the choir must conduct themselves reverently in the church, remembering that it is the house of God.

RULE 2.
All books and music must be handled and used with care.

As soon as the choir begin their duty of singing in the church, the following may be added :

RULE 3.
Every member of the choir at all services must conform to the ritual as prescribed by the rector.

RULE 4.
Every chorister must be in the choir room — minutes [5 or 10] before time for service.

The following, or similar, rules may be set forth as occasions may demand:

A

Regular attendance at practice is required; persistent irregularity without sufficient excuse will result in dismissal from the choir.

In one choir of my acquaintance, this rule appears in this shape: "Absence from three consecutive meetings of the choir will be considered equivalent to a resignation, unless such absence be caused by sickness, or when permission has been obtained from the choirmaster;" and closes with the significant words, "this rule can in no instance be deviated from."

B

Any chorister absent from the regular Friday [or Saturday] evening practice must not sing on the Sunday following without first obtaining the consent of the choirmaster [or rector.]

Another form of this rule:

No chorister will be permitted to sing in any service without attending the rehearsals for the same, unless specially invited to do so by the choirmaster before such service.

C

Profane or obscene language or conduct on the part of any chorister will result in instant expulsion from the choir.

This rule should never be set forth without cause. I never had but one choir in which it was needed.

Other rules will suggest themselves as occasions arise which demand them.

Common misbehavior should be punished by a diminishing of credit marks, or some such thing. For gross misbehavior in church, suspension from the choir for a definite length of time may be inflicted. For misbehavior at practice a reprimand is usually sufficient; if persisted in, suspension should follow.

Strict record should be kept by the clerk of the choir, not only of the attendance, but of the punctuality as well. For such purpose, the plan which I use, and which I have never seen outside of my own choirs, I have found to be a most excellent one. It is a method by which every chorister records his own punctuality, thereby making it a method of more than ordinary personal interest.

Every member of the choir has his own number. (After the choir is divided, it is a good idea to give one side the odd numbers, and the other side the even ones, even if it involves the changing of many numbers. They will often change, anyway). A double board opening on hinges, and provided with lock and key, is prepared, and set in some convenient place, having on each side numbered spaces—as many as there are members of the choir. Just under each number is a hole, and, on the left side, each hole contains a peg. As each member of the choir enters the choir room, for practice or service, he proceeds at once to this board, removes the peg under his number on the left to the corresponding number on the right. When the choir is called to order, the board is closed and locked. This gives the punctuality record, which is copied by the clerk into the record book at his convenience, before the next meeting of the choir. At the close of practice or service, after the closing collect in the choir room, the members of the choir call off their numbers consecutively, the clerk with pencil and paper in his hand calling off the numbers of absentees, marking them down as he calls them. This, also, he records at his convenience. The board may be made of such a size as to allow sufficient space on the right side to put a card under or over each number, bearing the name—and, in large cities, the street and number of residence—of the corresponding chorister.

The record, or roll book, should be properly ruled; a mark from left to right may be made for punctuality, and the reverse for attendance; thus:

No	NAME.	Oct. 7.	10	12 A. M.	12 P. M.	14	17	19 A. M.	19 P. M.	21
1.	JOHN BURNS.............	/	a	a	a	×	×	×	×	×
2.	WILLIE COOLEY	×	×	×	×	×	×	×	×	×
3.	ED. McINTYRE	×	×	×	×	a	×	×	×	\
4.	C. F. RILEY	×	/	×	/	/	/	a	×	×
		P	P	s	s	P	P	s	s	P

In this record, No. 1 was late on Oct. 7, and being absent on "the regular Friday night practice" (see Rule B. preceding), was not permitted to sing on Sunday, therefore was marked absent. On Oct. 21, No. 3 was present and registered, but did not answer in roll call at the close of practice, having been excused before practice was over. At the bottom of the page, P stands for "practice," S, for "service."

The hymnals should all be numbered consecutively, and each member of the choir should be provided with one, his hymnal number having no connection with his choir number. A chorister may, and doubtless will, find his choir number frequently changed, while the same hymnal should last him for years. This also serves to make each member responsible for the condition and care of his hymnal, as he will always use the same book. A list of hymnal numbers should be kept by the librarian, who should be the one to assign hymnals to new members of the choir.

CHAPTER XIII.

·

Training of Voice—Reading Music. ·

The training of the boy's voice resembles in many features the training of the mature female voice, while in many others they differ materially. Among the features of resemblance may be mentioned the need of patience and persistent practice.

It must be borne in mind that the natural and proper pitch of the boy's voice is the same as that of the female voice, an octave higher than the adult male voice. It may seem superfluous to insist upon this point; but I have heard more than one boys' choir in which the boys were *trained to sing in adult male pitch,* an octave lower than their own natural tone! Is it any wonder that in some rural parishes where the vested choir has been tried, it has been pronounced a failure? or that parents from such parishes have refused to allow their boys to enter a vested choir elsewhere, because they have known of boys' voices being utterly spoiled by such singing? Of course such choirs had no proper training, the clergymen were decidedly wanting in musical ear, and the choirmasters had probably never even heard a vested choir in their lives.

At first, boys should be taken separately, to secure proper and natural pitch. Sometimes it is well to have the assistance of a good, clear female voice; or, if this is not convenient, take one of the boys who sings in his natural pitch, to aid you in bringing up those who are inclined to sing an octave too low. First, sound middle C on the instrument, and then ask the boy to sing it to the sound of "ah." Then, the next note, and so on, up to F, or as high as he can sing. If he does not sing the tone in the proper pitch at any point, call in the assistance of the other voice, and tell the boy to sing it in the same manner. The average boy is quick and bright enough to catch the idea, and one such practice is generally enough for this purpose.

The boy's voice possesses two qualities of tone, which I find in my own experience is best understood by the boys themselves by terming them respectively "harsh" and "smooth," or "loud" and "soft."* After securing proper pitch, the "loud" quality of voice must be destroyed, and a clear, ringing, penetrating tone can easily be built up, based exclusively on the "soft" tones of the voice. The method always adopted by good masters is essentially as follows:

---

* Mr. Stubbs, following Curwen, calls them "thick" and "thin." See his book, mentioned elsewhere.

From among the boys who can not easily sing higher than

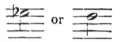 or

(treble clef understood), a sufficient number is first selected for the alto part, choosing those who display the most readiness in singing, and the best ear. Then train the sopranos and altos separately.

For the sopranos the following exercise is used:

ah, ah, ah, ah, ah, ah, ah, ah.

The first note must be sung softly, and with the mouth well opened—wide enough to place the forefinger edgewise between the teeth—to the sound "ah," as indicated. This will *invariably* be done with the "soft" quality of voice. Then ask them to sing the next note *just as they sung that one,* which they will likely accomplish with no great difficulty; then follow with the other notes in the same manner, keeping the "soft" tone throughout. If they break into the "loud" or harsh tone at about G or F, as they often will, try it over again from the beginning. This "soft" quality of voice *must* be secured as low as E. This exercise, repeated over and over again, both in class and separately, will bring about the proper quality of voice, so that all can produce it at will. *Never* allow a break into the "loud" quality to pass; if it occurs, the music must be repeated until it can be sung throughout with the proper tone. At first it must be sung softly, but after a while this tone strengthens, and at last develops into a clear, rich, ringing tone.*

The natural temptation to the alto is to sing the "loud" tone throughout. The altos should be trained in the same manner as the sopranos, beginning with as high a note as all can sing softly with ease; say

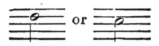

carrying that quality, as in the soprano, down to E.

I have, myself, usually permitted boys to use the "loud" voice below E, if they preferred, finding that in a very short time the voice regulates itself on the lower notes with but very little attention.

The next point is the development of the upper tones. In this it is necessary to proceed gradually and gently. After the voice is well settled in the "soft" quality, practice the scale of F *ascending,* retarding the time on the last four notes, and holding the last note; follow with the scale of F sharp; then, in very gradual succession, at different times, add consecutively the scales of G, A flat, A, and even B flat. This must take time. It is best to allow several months to bring a voice up to A or B flat.

The Altos will need special practice for development of the lower tones. A reversal of the above practice will accomplish this, beginning with the scale of B flat, *descending,* then following with the scales of A, A flat, G,

* I often find that it conveys the correct idea to boys to tell them that I want them to sing "like a woman."

G flat, and F. In all these practices use the sound "ah," and see that the mouth is well opened, the lips drawn back, and the teeth apart.

This is all the practice that is needed for the development of proper tone; but it should be constantly repeated, over and over again, at every meeting, until the tone is clear, pure and firm.

Some degree of flexibility must next be secured. This is best done by the use of the "Ten Exercises,"* which should be sung slowly at first, then with increasing rapidity, keeping the notes well separated, and sounding each one clearly.

The proper management of the breath must not be neglected. A practice of sustained tones is useful; directing that each tone be sung as long as conveniently possible, sing the scale of C, ascending. By frequent practice of this, the result will be all that is necessary.†
Be careful not to overdo this practice, either by singing too much of it at a time, or by trying to make each note too long.

Pay no attention whatever to critics who tell you that your choir has no power. This method of training will eventually bring power, and, what is better, it will bring mellowness as well, and make *expression* among the possibilities in singing.

Insist upon an erect position in singing. If standing, let the weight rest evenly on both feet, and, for an

* See Appendix D.   † See Appendix E.

occasional practice, direct that, before taking the preliminary breath to sing, each singer will make himself as tall and erect as he can without raising his heels from the floor. This has a tendency to ensure proper breathing. If sitting, never let boys stoop forward, with their elbows on their knees, or sit on the small of the back with their feet on the seat in front of them. An upright posture is the only proper one, and, while singing, it is best that the back should not rest against the back of the seat, but that the singer should sit a little forward.

Reading music should not be neglected. Some choirmasters never teach their boys to read, maintaining that boys will learn their music by ear nearly as quickly as if they could read. Although this is doubtless true, still, a choir that can read possesses a tremendous advantage. But it is not necessary that all should be *expert* readers before entering upon their work. All that is needed is a general knowledge of the first rudiments, the rest comes with practice. The different shaped notes and relative length of tones thereby represented, the different keys and their signatures, the effect of the three accidentals, and the various common marks of expression and movement should be learned, and all should be able to "call off" the notes by name in any key, and to read simple music.

Then begin with a combination of singing by ear and by note—*never* by rote. Do not allow the choir to attempt any piece of music, however easy, without the notes before them, to which frequent attention should be called.

First, select a very simple metrical hymn tune, such as
Dr. Mason's "Naomi." An opportunity here presents
itself for some preliminary instruction in phrasing; in
such a tune, the musical phrase corresponds with a line of
the hymn. Divide the tune into phrases and sections, as
follows:

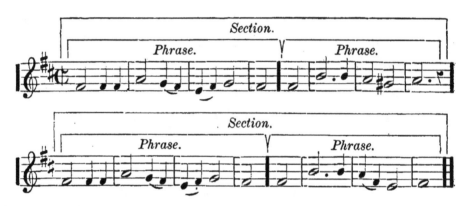

Direct the sopranos to sing the first phrase. We will
suppose that one boy sings the third note wrong, thus:

At once call his attention to the notes, and say to him,
"you can see that these three notes are all in the same
space of the staff, therefore they must be sung in the
same pitch; the third note is not higher than the second,
it is precisely the same. Sing it as it is written." Try
this over—singing the music with them—until the
soprano can sing it alone, and without the instrument;
then try the alto, tenor and bass successively in the
same manner, often calling attention to the notes. Then,
all parts together.

Then take the next phrase; and when this is learned, let each part sing the section—both phrases—once over, then together. Take the next two phrases in the same manner, and finally, the entire tune. Always use the verse set to the music, until the music is thoroughly learned.

In a short time, you will find it necessary to sing each *section* but once with each part, omitting the practice by phrases. And soon, by constantly referring the singers to their notes, you will find your choir able to take up new hymn tunes entire, at sight, and without this kind of work.

Chants may be learned in like manner, always using the *Gloria Patri* until the tune is learned.* Anthems and other set music will naturally follow. A very good preparation for fugal movements is some such metrical tune as "Northfield."

I have not considered it necessary to give a rudimentary course of instruction in reading music in this book. Any ordinary singing-school book contains enough for that purpose, and many choirmasters find a blackboard and crayon all that they require. The "tonic sol-fa" system of reading music is probably the easiest, but as comparatively little music is published in that system, it is not at all useful for choirs, and it is best to keep to the old method.

If your choir is of such a size that you can

---

* For hints on instructions in chanting, see chapter V.

do so, you should divide it into two choirs, for antiphonal singing, as nearly equal in power of tone, ability in reading, etc., as possible. In church—supposing the choir stalls to be properly arranged—the choir occupying the stalls to the left (facing the altar) is called the "Decani" choir; the other is called the "Cantoris." In processions, then, the Decani singers should take the left, and the Cantoris, the right, in going into the church. In returning, the reverse is the case. It is advisable to occasionally drill these two choirs in singing separately.

Boys should not be allowed to sing more than an hour at a time; or under exceptional circumstances, from a quarter to a half hour longer.

If not before, then shortly after the choir is fully organized and singing in church, arrangements must be made for filling the vacancies which are certain to occur in the soprano and alto ranks. The best method is to form a preparatory class, or "choir cadets," who will receive musical training, and from whom selections can be made as needed to fill vacancies. Some choirmasters, however, prefer to put the new boys into the choir at once, after a little preliminary training in proper tone, letting them sing only at practice, for some time, until they become quite familiar with the music and the ways of the choir.

CHAPTER XIV.

Admission of Choir — Processionals — Preparations for First Service.

Every member of the choir should be formally admitted to the service of the sanctuary. The form given in Appendix B, is a good one for this purpose. Whether the choir shall enter the church in procession for this purpose, or shall be seated promiscuously in the congregation until called up for it, whether it shall precede or follow some other service, whether such admission shall be public or private—all these and other kindred details must be left to local circumstances to determine.

In this country it is the usual custom, on occasions of public worship, for choirs to enter the church in procession, with singing, and often headed by a crucifer bearing the processional cross. The choir must have special training in this, for it differs vastly from singing in a standing or kneeling posture. First, the common and natural tendency to "keep step" with the music must be overcome. A choir clad in the vestments of the Church, keeping step, or otherwise marking the time of their singing, is not in accordance with Churchly usage or tradition. I have seen one or two choirs in which this custom was adopted, and it only served to impress me in favor of the Church's custom. The idea prevalent in such choirs is that of military precision, such processional hymns as "Onward, Christian Soldiers," "Go Forward, Christian Soldiers," "Am I a Soldier of the Cross?" encouraging the idea. It would be well enough, possibly, if a choir in such vestments could carry out this idea by keeping step; but, can they? do they? On the contrary, is not the effect rather saltatory than military, especial in "six-eight" time? Clad in military uniform it would be necessary; but robed in the vestments of the Church, it is incongruous—at times, painfully. Care should be taken, however, that the choir do not "straggle," or swing unevenly with exaggerated movements from side to side.

There are church buildings, small ones especially, in which processions are inconvenient, and even impossible. In such, the choristers should, as soon as vested, enter the choir seats—not necessarily in a body, but as they vest themselves, at their convenience—each, before taking his place, kneeling at the sanctuary rail and saying, privately, "Let the words of my mouth and the meditation of my heart be alway acceptable in Thy sight, Oh Lord, my Strength and my Redeemer," or some other appropriate prayer.

There is only one proper place in the church for a

vested choir, namely, the *architectural* choir—the space in front of the sanctuary rail. In some church buildings where a vested choir is to be introduced, this space is not sufficient as originally built, in which case it should be enlarged. The easiest way to do this is to extend it out into the body of the church, sufficiently to accommodate the singers, and, if possible, to place a light railing around it. The following illustrations will give an idea of this change, Figure 1 indicating this part of the church as originally built, and Figure 2, the same as altered for the choir.

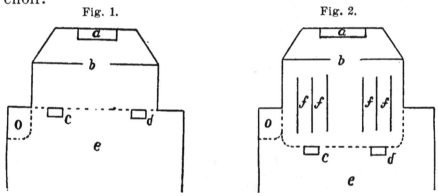

Fig. 1.   Fig. 2.

a. Altar.   b. Chancel gate.   c. Pulpit.   d. Lectern.   e. Body of church. o. Organ.   *f.* (Fig. 2.) Choir Stalls.

On entering the church in procession, the choir is formed with the Decani on the left and the Cantoris on the right; the crucifer (if there be one) leads the procession; following him are the sopranos, then the altos, the tenors and basses, the minister being at the rear of the procession. When the choir stalls are reached, the Decani turn to the left, the Cantoris to the right, and proceed at once to their places; the crucifer proceeds to the sanctuary gate, where he remains until the officiating priest takes his place, when he places the cross in its socket. The illustration given on the next page will explain this more clearly than can be done in words.

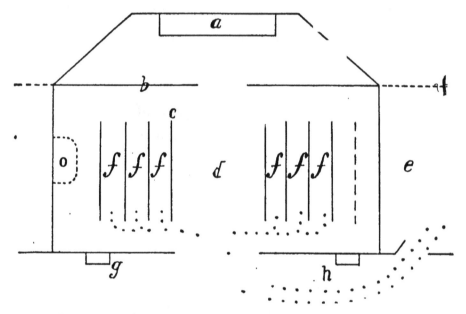

a. Altar. b. Sanctuary rail. d. Choir alley. c. Place for processional cross. e. Choir room. f. Choir stalls. g. Lectern. h. Pulpit. o. Organ The dots represent the course of the procession from the choir room.

Occasionally on some great festival, instead of proceeding direct to the choir stalls, the choir will go in procession up the side alley to the rear of the church, and then approach the chancel down the centre alley.

In leaving the church at the close of service, the crucifer, at the signal from the choirmaster, or in accordance with previous instructions, takes the cross from its socket, then, standing back a little space from the sanctuary gate, in the choir alley, faces the altar, remaining thus until the foremost choir boys are out of the stalls and facing him at the head of the choir alley, when he turns and leads the procession to the choir room. The choristers, it must be remembered, leave the choir stalls at the opposite end from that at which they entered, namely, from the end next the chancel. A "recessional,"* as this is usually called, should be direct to the choir room, and not around the church, even on festal occasions. In all processions care must be taken not to walk too rapidly, or to crowd together.

A simple service is advisable for the first one. Let us outline such a service; we will suppose it to be Morning Prayer, plain, and the Litany (preceded by a low celebration of the Holy Communion at an early hour, at which all communicants in the choir should have been present). For the evening, choral Evening Prayer. The hymnal, Hutchins.'

Previous to the service, the librarian should see that all music required for the service, except the processional, is placed in the racks of the choir stalls, a copy to each chorister, that the programmes are also distributed in like manner, that the number or name of the processional hymn is displayed in some convenient place in the choir room, and that the processional cross is in readiness.

---

* I know that the word "recessional" is often found fault with; but who wants to say "retiring processional," when a single word will do as well? Both are "processionals," to and from the church, but one feels the need of separate and distinct words for the two separate and distinct things. So by all means let us have both "processional" and "recessional," as both seem to be needed.

We will take for the processional, Hymn 232, which is vigorous, as well as easily learned. The choir, as they arrive in the choir room, after registering, proceed quietly to vest, get their hymnals, and then take their seats. At the proper time, the organist having been sent to the organ, they are directed to quietly take their places in procession. An opportunity then presents itself for any final instructions regarding the service; when all is in readiness, the minister, in a clear voice, intones one of the prayers suitable for such purpose,* to which the choir respond with the *Amen* on the same tone, in unison. This is generally sufficient intimation to the organist that the procession is ready to enter the church, awaiting his movements.

In some large churches, the choir room is at such a distance from the church, that the processional hymn can not be given out on the organ. In such a case, it is given out on the choir room instrument, which must, of course, be on the same pitch as the church organ. The choir, singing the processional hymn, enter the church as previously described. If the hymn is not long enough to last until all the choir are in their places, they should begin again at the first verse, and sing as much as is necessary. The same holds true regarding the recessional.

The *Venite* should be something simple, say, a Gregorian tone, sung in unison. No. 42 is excellent. According to the marking in Hutchins,' the first two verses and the

---

* See Appendix A.

Gloria are sung by the full choir, the other verses being sung antiphonally by Decani and Cantoris. Before the last note of one side has fairly ceased, the other side should begin the next verse. Nothing is so dispiriting in antiphonal singing as a long pause after each verse.

All should have the Psalter ready, and join heartily in the reading of the responsive verses, singing after each Psalm the *Gloria* to the same music sung for the *Venite* (No. 42).

The *Te Deum* may be more elaborate. Steggall, in A, is quite simple and forceful, as is also one by Garrett, in F. Van Boskerck, in F, is very musical, but presents more difficulties for a new choir than either of the others. Then will follow the *Jubilate,* or the *Benedictus,* which may be sung, in harmony, to a plain Anglican single chant (No. 99 or No. 119). Morning Prayer having been said, a hymn to a familiar tune should follow, and after the Litany, another hymn.

At the close of the sermon, the choir will rise, and after the Ascription sing the same *Gloria* that was sung in the Psalter (No. 42). At the presentation of the offerings, let the choir lead the congregation in "Praise God from Whom all blessings flow," to "Old Hundred," in unison. After the Benediction, a momentary silence, and then the recessional. After finishing the verse with which the rear of the procession enters the choir room, will follow the closing collect, said on the key (or its fourth) of the recessional hymn, the choir singing the

Amen; then should follow the roll-call, necessary announcements to the choir, and dismissal.

Each chorister should carefully put away his hymnal before disrobing, and the librarian should gather, sort and put away all other music used, should glance at the hymnal shelves to see that the hymnals are all in place, right side up, and should see that the cross is properly cared for.

At the evening service, the choir will proceed in much the same manner. The same processional hymns may be used as in the morning service, or different ones. The responses will be sung, and the chants will be those of Evening Prayer. It is best to read the Psalms, as in Morning Prayer, until the choir have had some little practice in their work.

In small churches, where the choir is small, and there is no opportunity for procession, this service must be somewhat modified. The choir, being in place before service begins, may sing their processional hymn, during which the minister enters. In the *Venite* (No. 42) the choir may divide for the antiphonal singing, the men singing one verse and the boys another. In the *Te Deum* no attention can be paid to the Dec. and Can. marks, save that some unison places may be divided between the boys and the men. Anglican chants must be sung full throughout, unless some such method as that described in chapter VII is adopted. After the Benediction, a hymn may be sung, during which the minister retires from the chancel, and, at its close, the choir withdraws in an orderly manner.

Each member of the choir should be provided with a programme of all music to be sung, in the order of the service. These may be written (a tedious task, however, for a large choir), or printed, or copied by hektograph or other copying device. The Edison mimeograph is probably the most useful, not only for this purpose, but for making copies of choir rules, constitution of choir guilds or clubs, music not otherwise available, and many other things.

The programmes may contain the order for morning and evening services on the same sheet, and should be prepared something as follows :

Sep. 7, 1890.

14th Sunday after Trinity.

Venite No. 42.

Gloria No. 42.

Te Deum, Steggall in A.

Jubilate No. 99.

Hymn 424—2d. Omit 2d and 3d verses.

LITANY.

Hymn 470.

SERMON.

Gloria No. 42.

Old Hundred.

Rec. Hymn 477.

Evening.

Service in D.*

Gloria No. 42.

Magnificat No. 176.

Nunc. D. No. 257.

Creéd, etc., in D.*

Hymn 439.

Gloria No. 42.

Old Hundred.

Hymn 336—1st 4 verses.

Rec. Hymn 477.

* See Appendix C.

CHAPTER XV.

Choir rooms and other facilities—General points.

A good choir room is one of the necessities. It should be large, well ventilated and heated, and adapted to convenience and comfort as well as utility. It should have closets or cases provided with "pigeon holes" for the keeping of music, most of which is octavo size—7x10 inches. To anticipate some slight variations from this measurement, it is well to make these little chambers eight inches wide by twelve deep, and at least three inches in height, for an ordinary sized choir. As soon as this music is purchased, before being used, it should be covered with strong manilla paper, and the title, key, and name of author should be written or stamped on the cover. The mimeograph is useful here, as one sheet of mimeograph paper will make a good many stencils for this purpose.

Some arrangement must also be made for the care of vestments, and their protection against dust; a closet built against the wall, with doors or curtains, will be sufficient. Hooks must be provided, and it is well to make the upper shelf low enough to allow of reaching up to it to lay a hat upon it. When the vestments are removed from the hook, the coat (and the hat, if necessary) can occupy the hook.

A Sunday School room, or chapel, can be utilized for this purpose, but it should be understood that the choir must not be disturbed in its use.

For practice, a good grand or square piano is the most useful instrument—never an upright, if it can be helped. But if a piano is used, the choir should have an occasional practice in church with the organ. Choirs should often be trained to sing without accompaniment. One of the proudest moments of my life was when my choir, new and inexperienced, carried through the evening service, choral throughout, with no accompaniment whatever, the organ having given way in the processional.

For the hymnals, a separate closet, or case, should be provided, with a compartment for each hymnal, numbered to correspond with the number of the hymnal, which should have its number *painted* on the back, and marked inside with ink. All members of the choir should be expected to take their hymnals from this case themselves before practice or service, and return them afterward; the librarian should exercise a general supervision over it, and report carelessness and neglect to the choirmaster.

Another necessity is a music fund, for the purchase of new music. In some parishes the evening offering is usually devoted to this use. Others apply the offering on.

a special evening in the month—the first Sunday evening, for instance. This fund is placed in the proper hands, and is under the control of the choirmaster. A very pleasant custom is to let it be known that donations will be very acceptable, a certain specified sum being sufficient to furnish the choir with a piece of music; and that any piece of music so furnished will be marked on every copy with the donor's name. This can be done on the manilla cover, when the title is placed there.

From this fund may also be paid an annual subscription to Hutchins' "Parish Choir" and Novello's "Musical Times," for the use of the choirmaster. When he sees in these periodicals anything he wants for the choir, the necessary number of copies can be ordered.

A metronome is a very useful choir property, both for practice and for reference. It can be set in a conspicuous place, at times, and the choir directed to follow its beating, thus receiving valuable drill in accuracy of time.

Reference has been frequently made, in the foregoing pages, to the processional cross and its bearer, the crucifer. In some parishes there is a prejudice against its use, which prejudice, I cannot but think, would melt away if those who entertain it could once understand its value to the choir, as a moral force. To boys—yes, and to men— it gives an added force to the expression, "soldiers of the Cross." It is, to them, what the regimental standard is to the soldier—it represents the cause in which they serve, and is a constant, eloquent, though silent, urging to worthiness in their service.

Let me add a caution here, which, perhaps, should have been introduced before, regarding the use of difficult music. Care should be taken that the music be not too difficult at any time. Nothing can be more disheartening to a choir than to attempt a piece of music and find it so difficult that it must be abandoned. The average choir led by an ambitious choirmaster is very apt to make this mistake, especially if the director's enthusiasm gets a little the better of his judgment. A choir of only ordinary skill and capacity will win golden opinions by confining their efforts to good music which is strictly within the limits of their ability to sing well; but when they attempt what is beyond their power, the public is very quick to detect it and to criticise such ambitious endeavors very harshly. The following extract from one of our Church papers is very worthy of attention :*

"Many choirs are *attempting* music that is beyond their ability, a course likely to bring boy-choirs into disrepute. The fault lies in a spirit of unintelligent imitation that seems to have infected the entire country, judging from the music lists, which show that incompetent and unskilled choirs insist upon attempting the most advanced and highly elaborated compositions. It is announced that a new Communion Service is to be produced in one of the churches of Trinity parish, New York, *e. g.*, and at once the publishers are flooded with orders for the same service. Now these Trinity choirs are under the direction of eminent masters in their profession, receiving sufficient salaries to enable them to give themselves wholly

---

* The *Living Church*, summarized from *The Chimes* the parochial paper of S. Paul's church. Buffalo, N. Y.

to their education and training. There are choral services during the week, and in one of them a daily choral service has been maintained for several years. The discipline and training in such choirs is consummate, and the delivery of important compositions intelligent and finished. The average village, or feebly sustained choir, on the contrary, receives limited attention, and often sings by rote. or in a purely mechanical way, and in attempting music of an exacting character, must lamentably fail, to the great discomfort and annoyance of the people. This line of counsel is capable of indefinite extension; although such is the blindness and self-satisfaction of .average human nature in all matters of æsthetic interest. that those who most need such counsels are very apt to construe them into occasions of offence, rather than of wholesome improvement."

CHAPTER XVI.

THE VESTED CHOIR.

Its Compensations: Salaries—Credits—Prizes—Medals—
Treats—Outings.

[Contributed by the Reverend C. C. Camp, rector of Christ Church, Joliet, Diocese of Chicago.]

The question of money compensation for a choir depends largely upon the financial ability of the parish. Where it can be afforded, a reasonable salary will be of assistance in securing the best talent and in enforcing regularity. Especially in large cities, where there is much competition, it will be found almost necessary to pay at least a few of the leading boys and men. But in most of the smaller places, and in many city choirs, few or none of the choristers receive pay, with the exception, of course, of the organist, and, usually, the choirmaster. The instruction, where there is a good choirmaster, is in itself a valuable compensation, and parents are glad, even when not particularly interested in the Church, to put their boys under such training and discipline. In some choirs those who join are required, on applying, to sign a promise that, in consideration of the musical instruction received, they will sing regularly in the services of the

Church for one year after their admission. The standard of the choir should be kept so high in music and morals, that membership in it would be eagerly sought and highly valued.

Where salaries are given—and in some cases where they are not—unexcused absences or serious cases of misconduct are punished by the infliction of fines. In this way, the amounts paid or withheld, while small in themselves, are helps toward the maintenance of strict discipline.

Where from motives of economy, or for other reasons, no salaries are paid—or sometimes in connection with the salaries—a system of credits may advantageously be used. Thus, in each choir, five credits are given for each required service, and when any chorister attains one hundred credits, he receives a prize or reward, usually in the form of some book. Under this system no credits are given for rehearsals, but in case of absence from rehearsal or service, or tardiness, or misbehavior, credits are deducted. The scale is as follows:

Credits given
For each required service..........5

Credits deducted
For absence from service...........3
For absence from rehearsal.........2
For tardiness.....................1

Thus, it will be seen that when there are two services each Sunday in which the choir is required, a chorister can obtain one hundred credits in ten weeks, not counting special days like Thanksgiving and Christmas. If however, he should be absent on Sunday, and from two rehearsals, he would not only fail to gain the ten credits that week, but would also lose ten that he had obtained before. Disorder or misconduct is punished by deducting one or more credits, according to the character of the offence. The prizes given under this system are not usually considered payments, but rather rewards. A money value, might, however, if it were thought desirable, be given to the credits—one cent each, or more—and thus make this system work as a part of a scheme of salaries.

The giving of medals monthly, quarterly, or annually for punctuality, reverence, and progress in music, acts as a strong incentive to the boys of a vested choir, and is quite generally practiced. The medals need not be expensive, and are usually engraved with the owners' name and the reason for which they are given. It is also well to have another medal, somewhat larger and handsomer, belonging to the choir, but worn for a definite period by those to whom it is assigned for general excellence.

In most parishes, there are special friends of the choir who will gladly provide little treats for them from time to time. These sometimes consist of a picnic or excursion, sometimes of a lecture or literary entertainment, sometimes of a pleasant social evening with refreshments. Such occasions are valuable, not only for their influence on the boys, in making them realize that it is a privilege to belong to the choir, but also in bringing the congregation into closer relations with the choir, and helping them to know the individual members.

If a choir club—such as is described in the next chapter—is organized in connection with the choir, such festival occasions may well be made to coincide with its meetings, and may help to bring together the active and honorary members of the club.

Chief among the compensations and rewards of a vested choir is an annual summer outing. This cannot always be obtained, but is of great value when possible. Preparations should be made long in advance; it is to be looked forward to, even during the winter, and often helps a boy to be regular at rehearsals when laziness says, "stay at home." It is a matter of considerable expense, which should be provided for in good season. Such expense ought to be borne by the congregation or parish, but the money is usually raised in part by a choir concert in the spring. The amount needed will vary according to the character, distance and duration of the trip.

An excursion from place to place, or boarding at summer hotels, will give much pleasure; but the best plan of all, both in good influence on the choir and in promoting their truest enjoyment, is to go into camp at some place where the choir will form a community by themselves. Some of the necessary qualifications of such a place are (1) proximity to a lake or stream where there is good bathing, boating and fishing; (2) good shade and suitable ground for pitching tents; (3) wood and water, —a spring, if possible; (4) considerable distance from any town or village.

This last provision may seem unnecessary, but it is really most important. The object of the encampment is that the members of the choir may learn to know each other, not that they may make new acquaintances. Far fewer rules will be needed in such a place than when near a town, discipline can be more easily enforced, and the religious services will be less interrupted. It will be a little more trouble to get provisions, but nearly all the provisions needed can be bought at wholesale and carried with the tents and baggage, while milk, eggs and butter can usually be obtained of farmers near by. It is well to buy sufficient lumber for a table and board seats.

Besides the general camp furniture, such as tents, cooking utensils, tin table-ware, etc., each person should carry a blanket or comfortable, small pillow or tick, bathing suit, towels, hair brush, comb, tooth brush, underclothing, stockings, handkerchiefs, soap, jack-knife, fishing tackle, and other personal effects. It is well to add, if possible, a rubber blanket or coat.

In most sections of the country, straw can usually be found in abundance where the farmers are threshing in the latter part of July or August, and a thick layer of this on the floor of the tent will make good beds.

For discipline, a light—but strictly enforced—form of a military kind is best, everything moving at the tap of the drum or the sound of the bugle. Rules should be few, but their strict observance should be demanded. Disregard of them may be punished by confinement for a specified time within certain limits, or in very aggravated cases of misbehavior, the culprit may be sent home. The following prohibitions have been found practically useful: (1) No fire-arms of any kind will be allowed; (2) swimming, bathing, boating, or going beyond a certain distance from camp must *invariably* be by permission of the rector or choirmaster; (3) no soprano or alto will be allowed to use tobacco.

The older members of the choir can be of great service in assisting the officers in the enforcement of the rules of the camp, and the intimate acquaintance of the rector or choirmaster with the members of the choir while fishing, bathing, eating camp fare, and playing games with them or telling stories at night, will add to his pleasure and influence throughout the year.

The expense of tents and camp equipage is considerable at first, but if they are used year after year, and a few articles bought each time, the total cost will not be burdensome.

A good cook is a most important personage in the camp—not simply one who understands cooking at home, but one who is enough of a woodsman to cook over an open fire. He will find that hungry appetites will give a fine relish to what he provides.

. It is well to take along a few simple remedies like Jamaica Ginger, Pond's Extract, quinine, paregoric and sticking plaster; but in a healthy, out-door life of this kind, there are not likely to be many serious ailments.

In regard to provisions, no general rule can be laid down for 'all communities ; but ham, bacon, salt pork, corn meal, griddle cakes, and syrup will be staple articles, as will crackers and ginger snaps. If fish can be caught, they will help out the larder.

There should be a brief religious service morning and night, and the singing of the *Gloria Patri* as a part of the grace before meals will be a pleasing feature in the woods.*

If a church is accessible, the Sunday services may be held there ; but otherwise a most solemn service can be held beneath the arching trees, to which the country people will come from far and near, if they know of it. A small portable cabinet organ is useful for this purpose, as · for many other occasions in camp when music is desired.

A choir going thus into camp, for. ten days or two weeks, will return home browned and tanned, strengthened and refreshed in body and mind, and ready to enter even more heartily into the service of God.

---

* See Appendix A.

CHAPTER XVII.

Choral Guilds—The Choir Club.

It is a very good idea to have some method by which the choir may be brought into closer contact with the people, either through their aid in music, or in a purely social way. The first may be accomplished by a Choral Guild, the second, by a Choir Club.

The Choral Guild need not be confined to parishes having a vested choir; it will work admirably with any form of choir. It should be composed of members of the congregation who sing, and the choir should be the controlling element. For instance, the constitution should provide that in matters under consideration before the Guild, if a division is called for, the majority should also comprise the majority of the choir, for the question to carry. It might also, in some cases, be best to provide that all—or certain—officers should be members of the choir. One advice I wish to give with the strongest emphasis possible, from the depths of my own repeated personal experience; it is this: *Never* make the conditions of membership so broad as to admit any one outside the congregation, unless it be a very few honorary members, not entitled to a voice or vote on any matter.

Meetings should be held with regularity, at least monthly, and oftener, if possible; at such meetings a portion of the time may be given to the practice of new Church music for congregational use, and some time may be given to the practice of English Glees and other secular music. This Guild may also form an "adjunct" choir, which, however, will be treated in the next chapter.

The Choir Club is of a different nature, its design being rather to furnish *social* recreation and enjoyment, and to bring the choir into closer contact with *all* members of the parish who choose to avail themselves of the opportunities given. It also brings into the choir a certain spiciness of variety keenly appreciated by all. It is under the auspices of the Club that secular concerts may be given, and all arrangements made for special treats and outings, leaving to the choir, as a choir, the music of the Church, and all matters pertaining thereto.

The structure of the Choir Club will perhaps be better explained by the following constitution, which is copied— with slight variations—from the constitution of such a society in actual existence in one of the larger parishes in the Diocese of Chicago, and of which parish it is one of the recognized institutions.

Constitution and By-laws of the Choir Club of ——— Church. ———, Diocese of ———

ARTICLE I.

NAMES AND OBJECT.

This society shall be known as the Choir Club of ——— Church, ———, Diocese of ———.

Its object shall be to promote the social, moral and spiritual welfare of its members.

ARTICLE II.

MEMBERSHIP.

Active:—Any member of the Choir, who has been a member in good standing for three months, may become an active member of the Club by signing this Constitution.

Honorary:—Honorary members shall consist of the following classes :

First Class. — Such members of the choir as have retired in good standing from active service.

Second Class.—Parents and wives of the active members.

Third Class.—Such persons as shall, for reasons satisfactory to the choir, be elected thereto.

Fourth Class.—Such members of the congregation as shall annually pay into the treasury of the Club such sum as the By-laws shall prescribe.

Nothing in this Constitution shall be construed as preventing honorary members of the first, second and third classes, from admission into the fourth class, if they so desire.

ARTICLE III.

OFFICERS.

The officers shall be a President, a Vice-President, Secretary, and Treasurer, who, with four additional members, shall constitute the Board of Directors ; the office of President shall always be held by the Rector of the parish, and that of Vice-President, by the choirmaster ; all other officers shall be elected by the active members.

ARTICLE IV.

DUTIES OF OFFICERS.

The duty of the President shall be to preside at any meeting of the Club or of the Board of Directors : also, at the request of three members of the Board of Directors, to call a special meeting of Club or Board, the object for which it is called to be stated in the call.

The Vice-President shall perform the duties of the President, in case of the absence of that officer or his inability to act, and shall have entire charge of the musical work of the Club.

The Treasurer shall receive the annual dues and all monies paid into the treasury, and shall disburse the same as ordered by the Board of Directors, or by the Club.

The Board of Directors shall have general charge of the affairs of the Club, and may be called together at any convenient time by the President.

ARTICLE V.

ELECTION OF OFFICERS.

A Secretary, Treasurer, and four Directors* shall be elected each year at the annual meeting ; but in case of a vacancy, such may be filled at any regular meeting. All elections shall be by ballot, unless ordered otherwise by a two-thirds vote of those present.

ARTICLE VI.

MEETINGS AND QUORUM.

The annual meeting of the Club shall be its first regular meeting in Advent. Regular meetings shall be held at least once each month, at such time as the By-laws shall appoint. Special meetings may be called at any time by the President. The Board of Directors shall meet whenever required by necessity or expediency of affairs.

At all meetings of the Board of Directors, a majority of the number—and at all meetings of the Club, fifteen active members—shall constitute a quorum for the transaction of business.

---

* In the Club of which this is, essentially, the Constitution, it is the custom to apportion the Directors to the four parts of the choir, electing one each from the sopranos, altos, tenors and basses.

ARTICLE VII.

DUES OF ACTIVE MEMBERS.

Each active member shall pay into the treasury such dues as shall be agreed upon by the Club, and set forth in the By-laws.

ARTICLE VIII.

AMENDMENTS.

This Constitution may be altered or amended at any regular meeting of the Club by a two-thirds vote of the members present. written notice of the proposed change having been given at a previous meeting.

BY-LAWS.

1.—Regular meetings shall be held on the first Tuesday of each month.

2.—Annual dues of active members shall be $1.20, payable entire or in such installments as each member may choose. Annual dues for honorary members of the fourth class shall be at least $2.50.

3.—The simplest methods of parliamentary usage shall prevail at meetings, the President's decision being final.

4.—When less than a quorum is present, and no officer, the members present may be called to order by any one of the number. and adjourned.

5.—These By-laws may be added to, altered or amended by the same method as provided in changing the Constitution ; but in adding new By-laws, this (No. 5 at present) shall be placed last.

CHAPTER XVIII.

THE ADJUNCT CHOIR.

[Contributed by the Rev. D. S. Phillips, S.T.D., Dean, and Rector of St. Paul's Church, Kankakee, Ill].

Wonderful has been the spread of the boy choir of late years in the American Church. Within the Diocese of Chicago it is stated that the increase of such choristers during the seven years preceding 1891 has been fully tenfold. Now, assuming that the boy choir has come to stay, it is pertinent to ask—what about the singing *girls* of our parish? Are they henceforth to be crowded out— their sweet voices no more to be heard in the service of song in the house of God? In the average parish we shall find twice, often thrice, as many girls with promising musical voices as boys. In the average Sunday School it is the girls that do the singing; the boys' voices, for the most part, cut no figure at all. Again, probably half a dozen girls are put to the piano at an early age for each boy; and so the theory of music is much better understood among them, and they learn vocal music more readily.

Said a teacher of music to the writer—a man who knew little of boy-choirs except by rumor—"It seems to me a great loss to leave the girls out of your choir, as you are doing -in the Episcopal Church. Girls' voices are more melodious than boys.' The feminine organization is finer than the masculine in childhood, as well as in mature years. Besides, girls take to singing naturally. You may get your boys to sing, perhaps, if you push them hard enough, but your girls will sing without urging, because they love it. And they would add a quality which would make the music of your boys and men a great deal better, too. Why, you might as well shut off all the soft-voiced, melodious stops of your organ, and use only the loud and strident ones, as to banish the girls from your choirs."*

But most clergymen and choirmasters, following Churchly tradition and usage, are decided in their objections to a. feminine element in the vested choir ; and, though it has been claimed in some quarters where this element has been introduced, that the music has been thereby greatly improved, yet the vested choir ordinarily means a choir of men and boys only, and is likely to retain that name in the future. But that leaves out all this rich and plentiful mass of musical material in our parishes, unless we can organize a girls' choir, as well as a boys'. More than that, the girls are likely to feel a sense of slight and injury ; they listen to the boy choir

---

* This quotation is worth two or three readings, as illustrating the erroneous opinions held by those who—as the writer says—know boy choirs only by rumor.—AUTHOR.

and believe that if they had the training bestowed upon the boys, they could sing better than the choir. *They* "would not make so many blunders as the boys did last Sunday in that TE DEUM, or Anthem !"

What, then, shall we do ?

Organize an "Adjunct Choir" of girls only, and let it be an understood part of the choirmaster's duty to train them well. You will find that it can be sustained with very little labor compared with what you expend upon the boy choir.

Let them even occupy the choir stalls at certain services when the vested choir can not be present—as for instance, the early celebration of the Holy Communion, or on Saints' days ; (and, perhaps, occasionally at a service for young people on a Sunday evening, let them sit in a body near the choir). They will lead the singing of the congregation, and, with a few bass and tenor voices that can generally be counted on, you will find it a marvellous improvement upon the general custom of no singing at all on such occasions.

It was a chance allusion to what the writer has himself attempted in this way that led the author of this work to request a chapter on the subject. "Write it all out—just how you do it," said he. The following scheme has only been in operation in my parish for three or four months, and perhaps it is too early yet to speak with much confidence ; but it promises so well that it is offered as an illustration of what may be done to utilize musical material among the girls in parishes having a vested choir of men and boys.

A society was organized under the name of "The St. Cecilia Guild," having the usual corps of officers, and permitting any girl in the parish from nine to eighteen years of age to be a member.

On approval of parents, an agreement is signed to be present at least twice each month, on an average, at the early Celebrations, and at such occasional rehearsals and Sunday evening services as the rector and Guild officers may decide. The membership of the Guild, at the present writing, numbers thirty-six; the average attendance at the early Celebration is about twenty.

Thus far, no change has ever been made in hymns or music—always the same, Sunday after Sunday, and nothing announced at the time of service. The Introit is Hymn 331, two stanzas, "Christ, Whose glory fills the skies." The *Kyrie, Gloria Tibi, Ter Sanctus,* one verse of a Communion Hymn—all sung to simple, familiar music. Hymn 203, "Thou God all glory, honor, power," has thus far been sung instead of the *Gloria in Excelsis,* and at the close, two or three stanzas of hymn 238, "Thine forever:— God of love," are sung. The entire service occupies from thirty-five to forty minutes. About one-half the Guild are communicants, and several of the remainder are preparing for Confirmation.

One result of having music at the early Celebrations has been to largely increase the number receiving (not belonging to the Guild), and it seems hardly possible that these young girls should be habitually present at this sacred service, joining reverently in the office, all close to the altar, without a solemnizing influence upon them more potent than any other public act of devotion in which they join.

Some such systematic encouragement of the musical young ladies and girls of a parish—where there is already a vested choir—to form a separate adjunct choir for special services, if given half the amount of attention bestowed on the boys, can hardly fail to produce certain very desirable and marked results:

First, a marked increase of interest on the part of the parish in services like the early Communion, Saints' days, or week-day evenings, at which the regular choir is never present. It would be found a great aid in the evening services of Lent. School girls cannot well be present on week-days, except in the evening; but at these, the "Adjunct Choir" would prove the most reliable of all helps, if expected to sustain the music.

Second, variety and additional interest in the music at special services for young people, on occasions of public catechising, or, as the custom is in some parishes, a monthly service for the Sunday School on a Sunday evening.

Third, in its effects on congregational singing. Scattered through the congregation, encouraged to sing with the choir in all music familiar to them, these members of the Adjunct Choir will often be found to do more for the congregational singing than their parents or elders.

Fourth, in those times of weakness to which all vested choirs are liable in our average or smaller parishes—when, perhaps, the voice of a leading boy has broken, and the soprano or alto is not "up to the mark;" the best singers in the Adjunct Choir will gladly fill in the deficiency, although not vested, or in the stalls.

If your experience should ever be like that of the writer, you will often hear members of the congregation say: "How much better the music is since the *girls* began to sing in the congregation so freely; *it never was so good before.*"

CHAPTER XIX.

The Rev. Mr. Clericus talks to his boys on "The Mistake of Ahimaaz."

EXPLANATORY NOTE.—The choir had begun to get a little unruly; even the best-behaved boys were becoming infected with the spirit of mischievous insubordination, and on this particular evening, the very atmosphere seemed to be surcharged with it. Suddenly, in the midst of the practice, the bolt fell; the rector, the Rev. Mr. Clericus, who was conducting his choir, stopped the practice in the midst of a phrase of music and sternly dismissed two boys, peremptorily expelling one, and suspending the other for a month. As this was the most severe case of discipline that had ever been exercised in the choir, it had an immediate and perceptible effect; the practice proceeded to the end with undivided attention and the best behavior. About fifteen minutes before the usual closing time, Mr. Clericus laid aside his book and baton, took up a small Bible that lay near, and after finding a place in the Old Testament* called the choir to order, and proceeded as follows:

---

* II Samuel xviii, 19.

I want to talk a little to the choir before closing the práctice this evening. Perhaps some of you were surprised at my action this evening regarding Fred and Harry. [Perceptible increase of attention]. While I do not think it wise in all cases—or even in many cases—to take the choir into my confidence in matters of discipline, there is such a valuable lesson connected with this one that I propose to let you all have the benefit of it. [Several of the boys exchange doubtful glances].

In order to impress this lesson on your minds in the best way, I want you first to carry your memories back to our "camping out" last summer [surprise]; more especially to the day we had the foot races; who came out ahead? Who beat? [Voices exclaim, "Ralph beat;" "Ralph won by six feet," and all turn to look at Ralph, who tries to appear unconcerned]. Yes, it was Ralph; and I remember how pleased you all were, even those that were beaten; because we all like Ralph; and, another thing, we know him to be very fleet-footed, and would rather be beaten by him than anyone else. And I presume you all remember how we ran the race over again with our tongues, around the camp-fire that night. [Subdued reminiscent enthusiasm].

But I think that Ralph would have been beaten if Ahimaaz had been there to run with him. [Questioning looks are interchanged]. Still, if I wanted to send a boy on an errand of any importance in a hurry, I would much rather send Ralph than Ahimaaz. [A hand is raised].

What is it, Jimmy? ["If you please, Mr. Clericus, who is Himmyaz?"] Ahimaaz? Why, did you never hear of him? [The boys shake their heads reflectively, and the tenors and basses begin to show signs of interest]. I am *sure* you have all heard of him; but I presume the one great affair that he figured in was so important and so interesting to you all, that you never gave him a second thought. But I think you will always remember him hereafter, for he had something to do with Fred's dismis-. sal from the choir this evening. [Perplexed whispers of "Who is he?" "Do you know him?" "Does he live here?" all of which Mr. Clericus ignores]. He had this to do with it—he made the same kind of mistake—not the very same mistake—but the same kind of one that Fred has been making ever since he came into the choir. And as I was thinking about Ahimaaz last week, and studying over him, it came across me that it was as unwise of me to allow Fred to sing in the choir, as it was in Joab to allow Ahimaaz to run a foot race with Cushi to see who would get to Mahanaim first. [Evident amazement in the choir].

I won't keep you in suspense any longer, boys. Ahimaaz was a young man in the days of King David, and we read about him in the Bible. He was the son of Zadok, one of the priests. You all probably remember the story of Absalom, the son of David; how he wanted to be king, and raised a rebellion against his father, and was killed by Joab, the commander of David's army, while he was caught by his head in an oak tree. A number of young men were there, and they took his body down and buried it. After it was all over, Ahimaaz came around, and, as the battle was over, he wanted to be sent as a messenger to David to tell him how the fight had ended.

As near as I can make out from the story, he didn't know anything about Absalom's death. But he was very anxious to go as a messenger, because he was a famous. runner; probably he could outrun anyone in the army. But Joab wanted to send the evil tidings of Absalom's death to his father by a more discreet messenger, even if he couldn't run as fast. So he said—and, it seems to me, in a very fatherly sort of way—"You must not go to the king with news to-day. Some other day I will send you with a message ; but not to-day, because the king's son is dead." And he turned to Cushi, who was probably one of the young men who saw Absalom killed, and said, "Go and tell the king *what you saw.*" And Cushi bowed to Joab, and started for the city of Mahanaim, where David was, on a run.

But Ahimaaz was a very foolish and impetuous young fellow. He was fairly quivering with excitement, and could not keep still, and he came back to Joab and said: "Whatever may have happened, do, please, let me run after Cushi." And Joab very patiently said, "What do you want to go for, my son; you have no message—no news at all."

But that didn't silence him. You see, he wanted to show Joab and every one else that he could run faster than Cushi, and ought to have been sent instead. So he finally wore out Joab's patience. "Let me run," he implored; and Joab, to get rid of his continual teasing, said, "Run." So Ahimaaz started, and in a short time he overtook Cushi, and beat him, and reached the king first.

All day long the king had sat at the gate of the city, and two watchmen had been up on the city wall on the lookout for any tidings. And now one of them comes to the king with the news that a man is running across the plain alone, coming toward the city; and the king said, "If he is alone, he must be a messenger; he has news for us." And then, after a while, Cushi came in sight, and the watchman reported that another man was running alone toward the city. And the king said, "He has news, too." You remember I told you that Ahimaaz was a famous runner? Well, the watchman knew him, and very likely had often seen him in foot-races, for he recognized him by his gait; at any rate he said, "It seems to me that the running of the foremost man is very much like the running of Ahimaaz, the son of Zadok." The king knew Zadok, the priest, and trusted him; so he said of Zadok's son, "he is a good man, and has good news." (There is in these words a hint of one reason why Joab did not want to send Ahimaaz to carry evil news).

When he came near enough, he called out a greeting to the king, and running into his presence, he prostrated

himself before David, and told all he knew in a breath :
"Blessed be the Lord thy God which hath delivered up the
men that lifted up their hand against my lord the king!"
This seems to be all that he was able to tell of the whole
day's battle. And the king was so anxious about his
rebellious son, Absalom! and he asked eagerly, "Is the
young man Absalom safe?" And all Ahimaaz could say
was, "When Joab sent the king's servant (meaning
Cushi) and me, *thy* servant, I saw a great tumult, but I
didn't know what the matter was." And so, for all his
eagerness to run, and for all his fleetness of foot, he
couldn't give the king any news at all, beyond the general fact that the king's army had won. So the king
commanded him to stand aside. And then Cushi came,
and by his discreet words, he justified Joab's choice of
him for a messenger.

Well, if I'm not careful, 1 shall run into a regular
sermon, and that is not my intention ; I want you to do
a little talking and a little thinking, too. Now, Ahimaaz
made a great mistake in this matter. What was the
mistake ? Put on your thinking caps, now, and tell me.
Frankie, what do you think about it ? [Frankie: "Was
it wanting to go to the king, when he didn't know anything to tell him ?"] Yes, that was it, partly. But there
was another, more serious one, underlying that. Who
can tell what it was ? Now, think hard.

[After a few moments' reflection, Alfred, a quiet,
studious-looking boy in the alto seats, says : "I think his

mistake was in thinking that he could do better than the other one because he could run faster"]. Right! that is it, exactly, Alfred. Perhaps it would be better to put it in this way: Ahimaaz made the mistake of thinking that the most important qualification for a messenger was his ability to run fast. That is an important qualification, no doubt: yet Cushi was the better messenger, though he could not run so fast.

Once in a while a boy, now-a-days, will make a mistake so much like that of Ahimaaz that they might be taken for twins—the mistakes, I mean; not the boy and Ahimaaz. The boy thinks that the only necessary qualification for a chorister is his ability to sing well. [Sensation]. That is the trouble with Fred. He has a beautiful voice, but he is irreverent at church, careless at practice, and discourteous—even impudent—at all times. He has a prettier voice than any of the rest of you, but I wouldn't give little Joe here for a dozen like him, although Joe has never sung a solo yet. [Great sensation, and Joe blushes to the roots of his hair]. Let me tell you why. Joe sings nicely, quite as well as the most of you, though not so well as Fred; but he is reverent and well-behaved. He is as full of fun as any boy in the choir, a good swimmer and ball-player, and we found out last summer that he could catch fish; but, above all, he knows how to behave; I never have to keep an eye on Joe.

Now a word about Harry. He behaved fully as badly as Fred this evening, and he has been doing quite badly lately. I suspended him for a month, and did not expel him, because he is only thoughtless, and has been influenced by Fred. The suspension will do him good.

And now, in conclusion, I want you all to take this lesson to heart. One day last summer, at the camp, I sat up on the bluff just over the landing-place, and saw Ralph and Jimmie and Alfred, and one or two more, get into the only boat that happened to be there at the time, and pull out from shore. Just as they had got out into the channel, Harvey came running down to the landing, and one of the boys in the boat called out to him, "Say, Harvey, your name is Dennis, this trip." [Laughter; blushes on Ralph's face]. Now, I simply want to say that any member of this choir who entitles himself to the name of Ahimaaz by falling into this mistake, will find it as bad a name as "Dennis." [The members of the choir evidently see the point and appreciate it].

But seriously, boys, consider the position you occupy as singers in the House of God. Think of the worship of God, as revealed to us:—the choir of holy angels falling down before Him, the blessed saints adoring Him, and we, unworthy as we are, being permitted to join "with angels and archangels and with all the company of heaven" to laud and magnify His holy Name ! How reverent we should be ! How careful in our lives ! God help us all, you and me, to be worthy of our high vocation !

APPENDIX.

A.

[Before Practice:]

Direct us, O Lord, in all our doings, with Thy most gracious favour, and further us with Thy continual help; that in all our works begun, continued, and ended in Thee, we may glorify Thy holy Name, and finally, by Thy mercy, obtain everlasting life; through Jesus Christ our Lord. *Amen.*

[After Practice:]

Lighten our darkness, we beseech Thee, O Lord; and by Thy great mercy defend us from all perils and dangers of this night; for the love of Thine only Son, our Saviour, Jesus Christ. *Amen.*

The grace of our Lord Jesus Christ, and the love of God, and the fellowship of the Holy Ghost, be with us all evermore. *Amen.*

[Before Service:]

Let Thy Holy Spirit be with us, O Lord God, that we may enter Thy courts with reverence and godly fear, and render a service acceptable unto Thee, through Jesus Christ our Lord. *Amen.*

or,

Cleanse the thoughts of our hearts, Almighty God, by the influence of Thy Holy Spirit, that we may worthily praise Thy Holy Name, through Jesus Christ our Lord. *Amen.*

or,

O Lord, our Strength and Help, may our services be acceptable in Thy sight; purify our hearts, quicken our spirits, and help our infirmities, that we may worship Thee in spirit and in truth, through Jesus Christ our Lord. *Amen.*

[After Service:]

Grant, O 'Lord, that what we have sung with our lips we may believe in our hearts and practice in our lives; through Jesus Christ our Lord. *Amen.*

or,

O Lord, make us more worthy, we beseech Thee, to lead the praises of Thy Church; and may we so worship Thee here below, that we may worship Thee forever hereafter in heaven; through Jesus Christ our Lord. *Amen.*

or,

Pardon, O Lord, we beseech Thee, the deficiencies and short-comings of this service in which we have been engaged, and be Thou with us as we depart from Thy house; for the sake of Thy Son, Jesus Christ our Lord. *Amen.*

[General:]

We beseech Thee. O Lord, to regard with Thine everlasting love, these Thy [children and] servants, who lead Thy people in the ministry of praise. May they worship Thee with undefiled lips and pure hearts, that their service may be acceptable in Thy sight; setting forth Thy praise, not only with their lips, but in their lives; by giving up themselves to Thy service, and by walking before Thee in holiness and righteousness all their days, through Jesus Christ our Saviour. *Amen.*

or,

[The prayer beginning "O Lord, Who in Thy wrath," at the close of the Service for the Admission of Choristers].

[The following "Grace before meals" will be found occasionally useful with choirs].

The eyes of all *wait* upon | Thee O | Lord: and Thou givest *them* their | meat in | due˙= | season.

Thou open*est* | Thine˙= | hand: and fillest *all* things | living˙ with | plenteous | ness.

Glory be to the Father, etc.

[Or, the *Gloria only* being sung to the above, the verses may be sung as follows]:

MINISTER.

The eyes of all wait up-on Thee, O Lord:

CHOIR.

And Thou giv-est them their meat in due sea - son.

MINISTER.

Thou openest Thine hand:

CHOIR.

And fill - est all things liv - ing with plen -teous-ness.

[Instead of the *Gloria Patri*, one of the following forms may be used:]

Supply the wants of all who are in need, O Lord, and give us grateful hearts for these and all Thy mercies, for Christ's sake.

[Or,]

Bless, O Lord, these Thy gifts to our use, and us to Thy service, for Christ's sake.

[to either of which the choir may respond:]

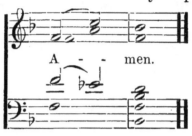

A - - men.

B.

Adapted from Bishop How's "Pastor in Parochia."

[The choir shall be fully vested for this service, save the candidate or candidates for admission, who shall be habited in cassocks, but shall occupy a place with the choristers].

Minister: Let us pray.

[Then shall be said—on any convenient tone—all kneeling, THE LORD'S PRAYER, after which all shall sing the following]

CONFESSION.

Holy, Holy, Holy, Lord God Al-might-y, Before Whom the angels

veil their faces, And in Whose sight the very heavens are not clean;

We confess that we are unworthy to speak un-to Thee. Pardon,

O Lord, all our sins, negligences, and ignorances, of the time that is past,

Forgive our wandering tho'ts, our heedless words, our oftentimes un-

wor-thy lives, And grant that, in time to come we may walk more

worthily of our holy office in Thy Church;

through Jesus Christ our Lord. A - men.

MINISTER. CHOIR.

O Lord, open Thou our lips. And our mouth shall show forth Thy praise.

MINISTER. CHOIR.

O God, make speed to save us. O Lord, make haste to help us.

MINISTER. (All standing.)

Glory be to the Father, and to the Son, and to the Ho - ly Ghost:

CHOIR.

As it was in the beginning, is now, and ever shall be, world without end. A-men.

MINISTER.   CHOIR.

Praise   ye the Lord.   The Lord's Name be prais - ed.

[Then shall be sung the XVth Psalm, as follows, during which the candidate or candidates will advance to the chancel gate, or the place appointed before the minister, accompanied by the choirmaster, or a chorister appointed to represent him].

ELVEY.

FULL. 1.—Lord, who shall *dwell* in thy | taber | nacle: or who shall *rest* up | on thy | holy | hill.

2.—Even he that *lead*eth an | uncor–rupt | life: and doeth the thing which is right, and *speak*eth the | truth·= | from his | heart.

CAN. 3.—He that hath used no deceit in his tongue, nor done evil | to his | neighbor: *and* | hath not | slandered his | neighbor.

DEC. 4.—He that setteth not by himself, but is *low*ly in his | own·= | eyes: and maketh *much* of | them that | fear the | Lord.

CAN. 5.—He that sweareth unto his neighbor, and *disap* | point- eth· him | not: *though* it | were· to his | own·= | hin- drance.

DEC. 6.—He that hath not given his *money* up | on·= | usury: nor taken re*ward* a | gainst the | inno | cent.

CAN.   7.—*Whoso* | doeth· these | things: *shall* | nev·= | er·= | fall.

FULL.   —Glory be, etc.

[The choirmaster, or his representative, shall then present the candidate (or, if more than one, each candidate separately,) with these words:]

I present A. B. for admission into this choir.

The minister will then give to the candidate his cotta and hymnal, saying:]

A. B., I admit thee as a chorister in this choir, entitled to its high privileges, and bound by its rules. What thou singest with thy lips, believe in thy heart and practice in thy life. And may God receive thee as a singer of the sanctuary in this world and in the world to come, through Jesus Christ our Lord. Amen.

[In the admission of a crucifer, the minister shall give to the candidate his cotta and, instead of a hymnal, the processional cross, saying]:

A. B., I admit thee as crucifer of this choir, entitled to its high privileges and bound by its rules. Ever bear this cross, the standard of the choir, with clean hands and a pure heart. And may thou so bear any cross that God shall lay upon thee in this world, that thou mayest wear a crown of glory in the world to come, through Jesus Christ our Lord. *Amen.*

[Then may follow a hymn].

[128, 176, 189, 422, 431, or 433].

[During the singing of the hymn, the new member retires, accompanied by a chorister appointed to assist him, vests himself in his cotta, then returns and takes his place as directed].

[After the hymn, the service closes as follows:]

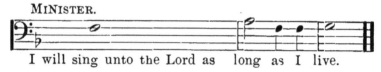

I will sing unto the Lord as long as I live.

I will praise my God while I have my be - ing.

[And the following Prayers:]

O Almighty God, Who out of the mouths of babes and sucklings art pleased to perfect praise; Mortify and kill all vices in us, that we may praise Thee with true childlike hearts. Give Thy special blessing, we beseech Thee, to Thy servants [or children] who have this day joined us in our holy office, and help them always to adore Thee with reverence and godly fear. Keep them, O Lord, from wandering thoughts, from lip-service, from vanity and irreverence, and from whatsoever other sin may most easily beset them. And make us all, we beseech Thee, examples and patterns to each other, and to the Church in which Thou hast placed us, that we may ever glorify Thy holy Name; through Jesus Christ our Saviour. *Amen.*

O Lord, Who in Thy wrath didst destroy Uzzah for irreverently laying his hand upon Thine Ark; Keep us, we beseech Thee, from our besetting sin of taking holy words irreverently upon our tongues. May we have grace to be always mindful of the solemnity of the work in which we are engaged; and may our reverence increase, as we become more familiar with Thy praises. Teach us to remember always how the holy Angels veil their faces before Thee. And may we so reverently praise Thee here, that hereafter we may with the Angels praise Thee in heaven; through Jesus Christ our Lord. *Amen.*

The grace of our Lord Jesus Christ, and the love of God, and the fellowship of the Holy Ghost, be with us all evermore. *Amen.*

C.

CHORAL SERVICE IN THE KEY OF D.

[Clergymen possessing deep bass voices often complain that they are unable to have a choral service, as Tallis' in G, or even in F, is beyond their power, they being unable to sustain the voice in intoning on that pitch with any degree of ease. It is for such that this service is com_posed. It is new, and at the present writing is used in two parish churches, the result in both being all that could be desired].

[The opening Sentences, Exhortation, Confession and Absolution may be said on any convenient tone, without organ].

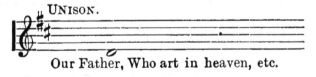

Our Father, Who art in heaven, etc.

O Lord, open Thou our lips. And our mouth shall show forth Thy praise.

* The minister may sing either the upper or the lower notes; the upper ones are a monotone on D.

MINISTER.

Glory be to the Father, and to the Son, and to the Ho - ly Ghost:

ANSWER.

As it was in the beginning, is now, and ever shall be, world without end.   A-men.

MINISTER.   ANSWER.

Praise ye the Lord.   The Lord's Name be prais - ed.

[Psalter, Lessons, and Canticles.]

UNISON.

I believe in God the Father Almighty, etc.

MINISTER.   ANSWER.

The Lord be with you.   And with thy spir - it.

Let us pray.

MINISTER.

O Lord, show Thy mercy up - on us.

ANSWER.

And grant us Thy sal - va - tion.

MINISTER.

O God, make clean our hearts with - in us.

ANSWER.

And take not Thy Ho - ly Spir - it from us.

(After each Prayer.)   (Final.)

A - men.   A - men.

D.

"The Ten Exercises."

No. 1.

(*Vocalize throughout.*)

No. 2.

No. 3.

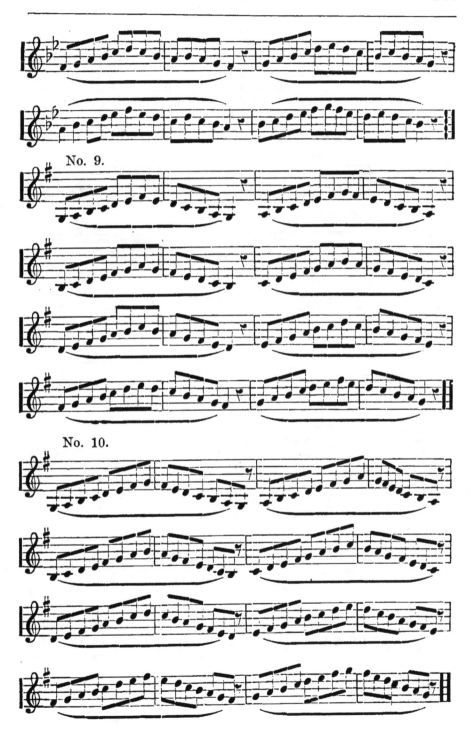

No. 9.

No. 10.

E.

(The following movement, from one of the choruses in the oratorio of the "Messiah," is not only useful as a preparation for the singing of that chorus, but for general practice in flexibility. Each exercise should be sung in a breath if possible, care being taken not to attempt too much at once, especially with boys.)

Movement from "For Unto Us."

No. 3.

F.

CORNET ACCOMPANIMENT IN CHANTS.

The cornet has been used with excellent effect in leading the congregation, in metrical tunes; but when chanting has been attempted it has been abandoned, owing to certain difficulties which *seem* insurmountable.

There is no valid reason why the cornet should not be used on the chants, if it is used at all. A proper method is all that is required. The following may indicate such a method to the intelligent cornettist.

First, all divisions of words, the breathing points, punctuations and italic (or otherwise marked) words to be prolonged, must be as familiar to the cornettist as to the singer.

Second, all these being familiar, discretion must be exercised in their observance.

The reciting note of the chant should not always be played, as on the organ, in one long, continuous tone, nor should the cornettist go to the other extreme and attempt to "tongue" all words and syllables. There is a certain intelligent and judicious method between these two extremes, which I will attempt to indicate by a setting of the "Venite;" the marks used will be intelligible to any cornettist.

NOTE: The method here outlined is useful also for piano accompaniment, with slight variations.

CORNET IN A.   Tone III—4

1.--O= | come let us *sing* | unto the | Lord: let us heartily re*joice* in the | strength of | our sal | vation.

2.— Let us come before His *pres*ence with | thanks·= | giv- ing‖and show our*selves* | glad in | Him with | psalms.

3.— For the *Lord* is a | great·= | God: and a *great* | King a | bove all | gods.

4.— In His hand are all the *cor*ners | of the | earth; and the *strength* of the | hills is | His·= | also.

5.— The sea is *His* | and He | made it: and His *hands* pre | pared· the | dry·= | land.

6.— O come let us wor*ship* and | fall·= | down: and *kneel* be | fore the | Lord our | Maker.

7.— For *He* is the | Lord our | God: and we are the people of His pasture, *and* the | sheep of | His·= | hand.

8.— O worship the *Lord* in the | beauty of | holiness: let the whole *earth* | stand in | awe of | Him.

9.—   For He cometh, for He come*th* to | judge the | earth:

and with righteousness to judge the *world* and the |

peo–ple | with His | truth.

Glo-ry be to the *Father*, | and to the | Son: *and* | to the | Ho-ly |

Ghost:

As it was in the beginning, is *now*, and | ev--er | shall be: *world*

without | end·= | A·= | men.